CHURCHES
That MULTIPLY

CHURCHES
That MULTIPLY

A BIBLE STUDY ON CHURCH PLANTING

ELMER L. TOWNS
AND
DOUGLAS PORTER

Beacon Hill Press of Kansas City
Kansas City, Missouri

Copyright 2003
by Beacon Hill Press of Kansas City

Printed in the
United States of America

ISBN 083-412-0437

Cover design: Ted Ferguson

Library of Congress Cataloging-in-Publication Data

Towns, Elmer L.
  Churches that multiply : a Bible study on church planting / Elmer L. Towns and Douglas Porter.
      p. cm.
Includes bibliographical references.
    ISBN 0-8341-2043-7
  1. Church development, New. 2. Church development, New—Biblical teaching. 3. Bible, N.T. Acts—Criticism, interpretation, etc. I. Porter, Douglas, Dr. II. Title.

BV652.24 T69 2003
254'.1—dc21

                                                        2002152651

10   9   8   7   6   5   4   3   2   1

Contents

Introduction   7
First-Century Patterns for Twenty-First-Century Ministry

1. The Greatness of the Great Commission   11
Jesus' Post-Resurrection Ministry

2. Witnessing: Key to Planting a New Church   26
The Disciples' Task

3. Saturating a Community with the Gospel   40
The Jerusalem Church

4. A Layperson Helping to Plant a Church   54
The Church in Samaria

5. Reaching Out to a Different Kind of People   68
The Church in Caesarea and Antioch

6. Plodding Through Problems with Purpose   81
The Churches of Galatia

7. Reaching Your Personal Sphere of Influence   92
The Church at Philippi

8. Building a People-Loving Ministry   105
The Church at Thessalonica

9. Building a Bible-Based Ministry   117
The Berean Church

10. Presenting the Gospel to the Secular Mind   124
The Church at Athens

11. Building a Ministry Team That Ministers   137
The Corinthian Church

12. Building People Who Build People   148
The Ephesian Church

Introduction
First-Century Patterns for
Twenty-First-Century Ministry

The Church is a living body. Just as everything that's alive will grow and reproduce, so your church should be growing and reproducing itself by starting another new church. Just as God originally created all living things to reproduce, that is, "according to its kind" (Gen. 1:11-12, 21, 24-25), so your church can double its ministry by planting another church. Think of a new church like yours that reaches new families, reaches a new neighborhood, and motivates new people to worship God in holiness.

Sometimes our denominational leaders make plans for new churches, and they organize to plant new churches. This is called the *trickle down* approach because a vision for new churches comes from the denominational top. But this book suggests a *bubble up* strategy, which means average Christians get a burden to begin a new church. Actually, both methods are biblical and both will work. But this book is aimed at giving you and many other members in your Bible study group a vision of how your church can start a new church.

Your study will cover the various church planting models in the Book of Acts and compare them with contemporary church growth principles. You will follow a step-by-step strategy of how your church can plant a new church.

1. Jesus' Post-Resurrection Ministry—"Strategic Planning"
2. The Disciples' Task—"Witnessing"
3. The Jerusalem Church—"Saturation Evangelism"
4. The Church in Samaria—"Layperson Ministry"
5. The Church in Caesarea and Antioch—"Crossing Cultural Barriers"
6. The Churches of Galatia—"Faithfulness in the Face of Problems"

7. The Church at Philippi—"Reaching People Through Relationships"
8. The Church at Thessalonica—"Ministry Born out of Compassion for People"
9. The Berean Church—"Ministry Grounded in the Scriptures"
10. The Church at Athens—"Understanding the Culture"
11. The Corinthian Church—"Spiritual Gifts in Ministry"
12. The Ephesian Church—"Leadership Training"

As you learn the various strategies and methods used in church planting, our prayer is that you will apply these Bible principles to your church. Besides learning church planting principles, you will be studying the Book of Acts from a new perspective, and you'll learn more about the Bible than ever before.

This book will involve you in *prayer assignments* so you will get vision and burden for a new church. Also, your class will be *surveyed* to determine attitudes, resources, and personnel for a new church. You will be asked to take some exploratory *trips* to new neighborhoods to look at potential areas for new churches. Some in the class will become involved in *coordination* with other classes in your church, other churches, and denominational leaders. Others in the class will *research* community plans and resources to determine where a new church should be located; that is, if your church is ready and able to plant a new church.

As you continue to study this book, a *vision committee* may be appointed to write a "Vision Statement" and/or "Ministry Statement" for the new church. Finally, your class may appoint a *coordinator* to work with your local church in its plans and actions for another church.

Perhaps your church is not ready to plant another church. This book will help make that determination. If you can't plant a new church, perhaps your church could assist another church with prayer and support as they take the initiative in church planting.

Get ready for one of the greatest adventures your class has

ever taken. Just as the Book of Acts contains exciting stories on new churches being planted all over the Mediterranean world, so you can continue that tradition in your community. And who knows, maybe the new church you help plant will be as great in evangelism as the Jerusalem Church, or as great in missionary outreach as the Antioch Church, or as great in Bible teaching as the Berean Church. We don't know what God will do through this new study, but let's give ourselves to studying church planting in the New Testament to see what God will do for us or through us.

Sincerely yours in Christ,

ELMER L. TOWNS and
DOUGLAS PORTER
A.D. 2002

1

The Greatness of the Great Commission

Jesus' Post-Resurrection Ministry

On the day of Resurrection, Jesus appeared to several individuals, for example, Mary Magdalene in the garden, Peter at an unknown location, the couple on the road to Emmaus, but His most significant appearance was in the Upper Room to 10 disciples. The doors were barred and the windows were shut, then suddenly, without warning, Jesus appeared in their midst. "Peace be with you" (John 20:19) was the first thing He said to them. Obviously, the disciples were excited, but they were also curious. They wanted to know about His wounds and if He was really physical. Then Jesus "showed them His hands and His side. Then the disciples were glad when they saw the Lord" (v. 20). Later "they gave him a piece of a broiled fish, and of an honeycomb. And he took it, and did eat before them" (Luke 24:42-43, KJV).

There were probably many things the disciples wanted to talk about, and in God's perspective, there were many things they needed to know. But the primary reason Jesus met them in the Upper Room was to give them the Great Commission.

In the Great Commission Jesus gave them His authority, just as He received authority from the Father. But notice what Jesus left out the first time He gave them the Great Commission. Jesus did not tell them where to go, what to do, what to

The First Communication of the Great Commission

"As the Father has sent Me, I also send you" (John 20:21).

preach, or what accomplishments they would have. The first time Jesus just gave them a *command;* they were to go just as He had gone.

The Second Communication of the Great Commission

"And He said to them, 'Go into all the world and preach the gospel to every creature'" (Mark 16:15).

A week later the disciples were again in the Upper Room (John 20:26), but this time there were 11 disciples (Mark 16:14), whereas only 10 disciples were there the first time (Judas was dead and Thomas was hiding). We know the meeting described in Mark is Jesus' next physical appearance to them. Thomas the doubter was not there the first time but is now with them (John 20:24-29). Even though the disciples saw Him seven days earlier, and even though He is talking with them now, they still have trouble with unbelief: "They did not believe" (Mark 16:14).

That's a picture of many people today; they know they are saved, and they have been converted, but they still struggle with unbelief. Like the disciples, they love the Lord and obey Him, but they have a little nagging doubt of unbelief.

In the second encounter with the disciples, Jesus added the Great Commission. He added the *purpose* for their going, and where they should go. "Go ye into all the world, and preach the gospel to every creature" (Mark 16:15, KJV).

The disciples may have had some misconceptions because of what Christ didn't say. The first time He gave them the Great Commission. They could have thought He was sending them back to Galilee. They could have thought He was sending them to minister to the Jews. They could have thought their ministry was a repetition of what Jesus did, that is, traveling from city to city to tell the good news of the kingdom of heaven.

This second time Jesus removed any doubts in their mind about where they should go and what they should do. They were to go into all the world, not just to Galilee or be limited to the Holy Land. They were to preach the gospel to every person in the world, not just to the Jews.

Is your church thinking about planting another church? That could include going to a new neighborhood and sharing the gospel with every person in that neighborhood. That could be passing out literature from door to door, posting the gospel on a web site, printing the gospel in a local newspaper, buying local television or radio time to share the gospel, or any other means of publicizing the gospel by media. Obviously, that would mean going to every home in a new neighborhood and reaching every person in a new neighborhood. Planting a new church means saturating a new neighborhood with the gospel.

Jesus met His disciples this third time, probably one week later on a mountain in Galilee (Matt. 28:16). This hill may have been right outside Capernaum, the city that had been home base for Jesus' ministry for the last three years. The mountain was probably where Jesus had frequently met with the disciples, teaching and ministering.

When Jesus appeared to them, "they worshiped Him" (v. 17). Because Jesus could appear at any place, they knew He was God. Because He had been resurrected from the dead, they knew He was their living Messiah. Because He came to them again, they were grateful and showed it in worship.

The Third Communication of the Great Commission

"Go therefore and make disciples of all the nations, baptizing them in the name of the Father and of the Son and of the Holy Spirit, teaching them to observe all things that I have commanded you; and lo, I am with you always, even to the end of the age" (Matt. 28:19-20).

Jesus again expanded the Great Commission. This time He gave them authority: "All authority has been given to Me in heaven and on earth" (v. 18). That meant that Jesus had the authority of the Father and the Holy Spirit to give to them. He added to the Great Commission the promise, "I am with you always, even to the end of the age" (v. 20). So His authority went with them, because He was with them. But that means when we carry out the Great Commission, we have His authority to plant a new church because we have His presence with us.

Then Jesus again added three more steps to their task. "Go therefore and make disciples of all the nations, baptizing them in the name of the Father and of the Son and of the Holy Spirit, teaching them to observe all things that I have commanded you" (vv. 19-20).

Notice the first step included "make disciples of all the nations." Their task was more than just preaching to people; they were to get results. Their task now included winning people to faith and discipling each convert so that they follow Jesus, just as the Eleven followed Jesus. Therefore when you carry out the Great Commission, you must fulfill a discipling commission. When you win someone to Jesus Christ, you are to follow up that person with teaching, encouragement, and motivation, so that each new convert will follow Jesus as you follow Jesus. Just as Jesus went through Galilee asking people to follow Him, now you should go to a new neighborhood to ask people to follow Jesus.

Perhaps as Simon and Andrew were listening to Jesus, they remembered the day He walked along the shore of Galilee to offer, "Come after Me, and I will make you fishers of men" (Mark 1:17). Perhaps Matthew the tax collector remembered sitting at his collection table when Jesus passed by to say, "Follow Me" (Mark 2:14).

The second step of the Great Commission was on "the nations." The Greek word for "nations" is *ethnē*, that is, "people groups." Jesus focuses their attention on the ethnic groups or people groups of the world. When the Bible says, "For God so loved the world" (John 3:16), it includes every person and every people group in the world. So Jesus was telling His disciples to go to every people group and make disciples within that group of people.

Too often we read the King James Version of the Bible and think the words "the nations" mean a political or social group of people called a nation, such as members of the United Nations. But the Great Commission is much more explicit than political nations. Its focus is people groups, or ethnic groups. Think of all the people groups within the United States, for example, African-Americans, Irish-Americans, Indian-Americans, Chinese-Americans, and then look at a different distinction, for example, southern hill people, urban dwellers, street people, third-generation people of Mexican descent living in Texas, illegal Mexicans in California, and Spanish-Americans who have always lived in the Southwest. Jesus is directing the Church to make disciples of every people group in the world.

Think of some neighborhood that your church should reach with the gospel. Who lives in that neighborhood? How many different people groups live in that neighborhood? Could you start one church among a specific people group? Or should you start a church that incorporates several different people groups? Obviously that's a question that you can't answer without more information. Therefore, to plant a church, you will want to survey your neighborhood to find out who is there. Just as a successful company will survey its potential customers to find out what customers want and need, so a successful church plant should survey a neighborhood to find out who is there, because that determines how we reach out to them with the gospel to win them to Jesus Christ.

On the 40th day after His resurrection, Jesus added more to the Great Commission. He had previously told the disciples to go to all people in the world, the fact that they should preach, and that they should disciple every new convert. Now on the 40th day, Jesus summarized the content of their preaching.

The Fourth Communication
of the Great Commission

"Then He said to them, 'Thus it is written, and thus it was
necessary for the Christ to suffer and to rise from the dead
the third day, and that repentance and remission of sins
should be preached in His name to all nations, beginning
at Jerusalem. And you are witnesses of these things'"
(Luke 24:46-48).

He met with His disciples in Jerusalem. We don't know where in the city they were meeting, nor do we know any of the details when He met them. But we do know that after telling them what content to preach, "He led them out as far as Bethany" (Luke 24:50). When they got to Bethany, "He lifted up His hands and blessed them" and was "carried up into heaven" (vv. 50-51).

But in the city of Jerusalem, Jesus instructed them what to preach. He said, "Thus it is written, and thus it was necessary for the Christ to suffer and to rise from the dead the third day" (v. 46). The content is the gospel, that is, the death of Jesus Christ for our sins and the resurrection of Jesus Christ to give us new life (1 Cor. 15:1-4).

Obviously, the disciples did not understand the substitutionary nature of Jesus' death as He hung on the Cross. All they could think of was the physical suffering of the One they loved. They did not see the Cross theologically; nor did they understand the ramifications of redemption, that is, Jesus was paying the price for sin. They did not immediately understand that the blood of Jesus Christ, God's Son, cleanses from all sin (1 John 1:7). All they understood was that Jesus died. However, during the 40 days on earth, Jesus explained the doctrinal meaning of the Cross and His death. Now on the last day before returning to heaven, Jesus instructs them to preach His death and resurrection as they go into all the world.

And what should be the response of the listeners to the

message of His death and resurrection? Jesus instructed them, "That repentance and remission of sins should be preached in His name to all nations, beginning at Jerusalem" (Luke 24:47). They are to preach *repentance;* it's a simple word that means "to change the mind." The people were to change their minds about sin, to change their minds about their life's pursuit, and when they changed their inner minds, they were to change their actions. They were to turn around and leave sin, to follow Christ. So on the Day of Pentecost, Peter preached a strong message of repentance. "Repent, and let every one of you be baptized in the name of Jesus Christ" (Acts 2:38).

But Jesus also included more in their task of preaching on that 40th day. He told His disciples, "You are witnesses of these things" (Luke 24:48). Just as a witness must share what he has seen, heard, and experienced, the disciples were to share with every person in the world their experiences with Jesus Christ.

So when you go to begin a new church in a new neighborhood, what message should you share with the recipients? You should tell them that Jesus died to forgive their sins, and that He rose from the dead to give them new life. This is first and foremost your message. Don't get caught up in secondary things such as teaching people how to have a good family, how to live successfully, or how to be overcome problems. All these are good and have their place, but God does not want you to teach these things apart from the gospel. Remember, when you plant a church, you have a primary message of redemption to the people in the new community. That's the gospel of Jesus Christ, which can save them from sin.

On four previous occasions Jesus had told the disciples to go evangelize the world, each time adding more details to the Great Commission. Now He's ready to leave; they walk out of the city of Jerusalem to the Mount of Olives near the city of Bethany. As Jesus is poised to leave them, He repeats the Great Commission a fifth time. But even this last time He added more details. Jesus adds geography. But not just geographical destinations; He adds geographical strategy. The disciples are to begin in Jerusalem. He has already told them to go into Jerusalem to pray until the Holy Spirit comes upon them. The disciples did not understand what power they would receive when the Holy Spirit came, nor did they have any idea of the results they would have in the city of Jerusalem. But they were to begin preaching in Jerusalem.

The Fifth Communication of the Great Commission

"But you shall receive power when the Holy Spirit has come upon you; and you shall be witnesses to Me in Jerusalem, and in all Judea and Samaria, and to the end of the earth" (Acts 1:8).

And what does Jerusalem mean to the Twelve? It means that they are not to break up to go individually into the world. Jesus does not want His disciples to be splintered, but to stay in Jerusalem until there is a solid foundation from which the Church can reach out into the whole world. And what else does He say? He doesn't want them running to the end of the world and bypassing anyone on the way. They are to leave Jerusalem and reach out into Judea. Then they are to go to Samaria, the next closest group of people, and finally to the ends of the earth. Therefore, the Great Commission would be fulfilled in a gradual manner, in a planned sequence, including all people, overlooking none, systematically and continually preaching the gospel, until they go to the end of the world. This strategy would have a solid base in Jerusalem, so that's where they were to begin.

What can you learn about church planting in a near neighborhood? First, there must be a strong *mother church,* that will send out and plant a *daughter church.* Just as the Jerusalem church became the pattern and strength of every daughter church that it planted, so your mother church will share its strength, passion, and vision.

Whereas some Christians may think that it will harm a mother church to give some of its members to plant a daughter church, the Scriptures say, "Give, and it shall be given unto you" (Luke 6:38, KJV). History has witnessed that mother churches become stronger when they give their members to plant new churches.

The Need for Strategy

The fact that Jesus had a strategy to the Great Commission shows that God had a very definite plan and purpose for extending His ministry to the world. He didn't leave His work for people to invent what they thought was best, nor did He leave them in frustration with the great command, not knowing how to carry it out. Just as God had a strategy for reaching the world, so He has a strategy for reaching the unreached communities around your church. That means you shouldn't be frustrated with great amounts of people in your area that are unsaved. God has a strategy to reach them; it includes you and your church.

When Jesus gave the Great Commission, He did not send us out alone. Sometimes a sales manager will send a salesperson on the road. And that isolated salesperson has to make it by his own initiative and inventiveness. When the salesperson faces an insurmountable task, he or she simply fails. But Jesus sent His disciples to preach the gospel in the entire world; He promised to be with them. When they faced an insurmountable witnessing problem, He promised to be with them to help them. When they faced loneliness or discouragement, He promised to be with them for encouragement. Therefore, as you think of planting a new church, remember Jesus will be with you because He indwells every believer on the ministry team. Also, Jesus will be with you because He said, "Where two or three are gathered together in My name, I am there in the midst of them" (Matt. 18:20).

Also, when Jesus sent His disciples out, He promised them power. All they had to do was wait and pray for God to supply the power. Isn't it good to know that as you plant a new church, God will give you power to make it happen? The success of a new church is not something you have to worry about or strive for. The Lord has promised to give you power as you go, so your responsibility is to "go," and God's responsibility is to supply the power.

When Jesus ascended to heaven, only 120 retreated to the Upper Room to pray, to seek God's face, and to wait for something they were promised but didn't quite know what it would be. They were waiting for the Holy Spirit. If an objective observer had been asked if the small remnant would survive, he'd probably have said "no!"

After all, this tiny band of revolutionaries had lost their earthly leader. They were persecuted by the religious governing body, the Jews. They were oppressed by the world rulers, the Romans, because they refused to worship Caesar. Their lifestyle was rejected by society because they didn't worship idols, drink alcoholic beverages, and participate in immoral sexual practices. Besides all that, Satan trained all the weapons of hell against them because he knew—if this small group of Christians were successful—they could eventually capture followers from among the entire human race.

The small group of 120 multiplied to 3,000 . . . then 5,000 . . . then multitudes. The single group of 120 multiplied to many groups, then those groups—called churches—spread over the Roman Empire until their opponents said, "These that have turned the world upside down are come [here] also" (Acts 17:6, KJV).

How did the explosion of Christianity take place? First, God was on their side, and He was more than just One among them; God was their power, their passion, and the supreme object of their worship. Because those Christians experienced a supernatural conversion, they knew they were right. And there is might in those who are right. These Christians were willing to give their lives for the One who died for them; therefore death had no sting to them, and suffering didn't faze them.

The Power of Community

Christianity always is personal, for God saves people one at a time. Each person expressed personal faith, and each person was individually accountable to God. But Christianity did not spread just through individuals; it spread through their churches. God's strategy was the community, also called the Body of Christ (Eph. 1:22-23). Christians went everywhere planting churches, and each newly planted church became a powerful center of evangelistic outreach into the community. Eventually, believers in each new church planted another one. Christians took refuge in their church and also received strength from it because Jesus was there. He said, "Where two or three are gathered together in my name, there am I in the midst of them" (Matt. 18:20, KJV). Each local group of Christians was reflective of the universal Body of Christ in heaven to which all believers of all ages belonged. All believers had the living Christ individually in them, but they also believed they had His power to do exploits.

These churches were loving bodies where all persons loved one another because they all loved Jesus. Therefore, those churches had strength because all received love as they gave it to others. Those churches were also sacrificing bodies because all members gave their time, talent, and earthly treasures to serve Jesus Christ. If ever there was a group that meant, "All for one and one for all," it was those original New Testament churches.

Those churches were praying churches. They touched God, who in turn answered their prayers. Each new church was born in prayer and advanced on the knees of praying Christians. In prayer, they fellowshipped with God, worshiped God, and interceded for the salvation of lost people. Those who were saved joined the local body as equal members who in turn had access to all of the privileges of those who originally heard the actual words of Christ.

Personal Lessons to Take Away

1. I can help carry out the Great Commission by individual witnessing and by helping plant a new church.

2. I can share the gospel with lost people, which is the only message that will give them eternal life.

3. I can witness my faith to lost people, sharing with them my salvation experience.

4. I can be part of a new church plant that would place me at the center of carrying out the Great Commission.

Church Lessons to Take Away

1. A church becomes actively involved in carrying out the Great Commission when it plants another church.

2. Churches should have a systematic and sequential plan to continually preach the gospel to all people, including both home and foreign missions.

3. Churches are the natural outcome when the Great Commission is carried out.

4. Churches obey the last command of Christ when they plant a new church to evangelize an unreached area.

Personal Project

The Great Commission was given to the disciples, but it applies to us today. Ask yourself, "What is my task in completing the Great Commission?" Use the following personal project:

Commandment Assessment. Study the different times Jesus communicated the Great Commission to determine what you are doing about it and, more importantly, what you are willing to do about it.

   a. John 20:21: "So send I you" (KJV). You have a commission to obey Jesus by going wherever He sends you. Are you willing to go wherever He sends you?

   b. Mark 16:15: "Go . . . preach the gospel to every creature." You have a task. Are you willing to share the gospel with anyone—no matter who they are—that crosses your daily life?

   c. Matt. 28:19-20: "Go . . . make disciples . . . baptizing them . . . teaching them." Are you willing to become part of a ministry team that will go evangelize people by planting a new church?

d. Acts 1:8: "You shall be witnesses . . . in Jerusalem, and in all Judea and Samaria, and to the end of the earth." Jesus gave us a geographical strategy to evangelize the world, starting at Jerusalem, which represents our home. Are you willing to begin at your home church and follow the Lord's leading to reach out in a church plant?

Church Project

The Bible teaches that Christians are to reproduce Christians, and churches are to reproduce churches. Your church should begin a 12-week process of studying if it should start a new church.

1. *Strategic Planning Group.* Make the present class study this series, or form a ministry team that will study the following questions:

   a. Is our church spiritually prepared to begin a new church? (If not, why not?)

   b. Is there a natural neighborhood nearby that would be the appropriate place to begin a new church? (Where, why?)

   c. What should happen before our church starts a new church?

   d. What are some of the steps necessary for our church to start a new church?

   e. What is a suggested timeline that would be necessary for us to follow in planning for a new church plant?

2. *Vision Statement.* In order to begin a new work, a group should have a vision or dream of what they want to accomplish. The educational world describes this in terms of learning objectives or teaching goals. The business world has a statement of purpose or objective. In the church we use the term *vision statement,* because a vision is not something we work up from our thinking. A vision is given to us by God.

Try to begin writing a *vision statement*. The following vision statement was written by Rick Warren while the new church he was starting met in the living room of a private dwelling. This statement is not given for your church to copy but is given as an illustration to give you creativity and composition.

The Saddleback Vision

It is the dream of a place where the hurting, the hopeless, the discouraged, the depressed, the frustrated and confused can find love, acceptance, help, hope, forgiveness, guidance and encouragement.

It is the dream of sharing the Good News of Jesus Christ with the hundreds of thousands of residents in south Orange County.

It is the dream of 20,000 members growing together in spiritual maturity through Bible studies, seminars, retreats, and fellowship—loving, laughing, and learning together, understanding God's wonderful plan and living life to its greatest potential.

It is the dream of sending out hundreds of career missionaries and church workers all around the world, and sending out our members by the thousands on short-term mission projects to every continent. It is the dream of starting at least one new daughter church a year.

It is the dream of 50 acres of land, on which will be built a regional church for southern Orange County—with beautiful yet efficient facilities . . . including a worship center seating thousands, counseling and prayer center, classrooms for Bible study and training lay ministers, and a professional aerobics recreational center. All of this will be designed to minister to the total person—spiritually, emotionally, physically and socially—and set in a peaceful, inspiring garden setting with bright flowers, beautiful trees, and pools of still water, sparkling fountains, and flowing streams. I stand before you today and state in confident assurance that these dreams will be realized. Why?

Because They Are Inspired By God
From Pastor Rick's First Sermon
March 30, 1980[1]

3. *Form Ministry Team.* The ministry team needs to begin meeting together to form a sense of identity or community. They could eventually form a separate Sunday School class or separate prayer meeting. Sometimes the ministry team will meet in the mother church for six months to a year. During this time, they can begin studying the area, research scriptures, survey the mother church, and so forth. (There are projects at the end of each chapter to guide the ministry team as they grow toward becoming a new church.) The ministry team may begin to organize by doing the following:

   a. Appoint a team leader (doesn't have to be the new pastor, or even a board member from the mother church or the new daughter church).

   b. Appoint a secretary to carry on correspondence and keep any official letter/correspondence/and so forth.

   c. Appoint a treasurer to oversee the money for the new church.

   d. Appoint a prayer leader to guide prayer projects.

   e. Appoint a group to oversee advertisement and publicity.

---

1. Elmer Towns, *10 Sunday Schools That Dared to Change* (Ventura, Calif.: Regal Books, 1993), 73.

2

Witnessing: Key to Planting a New Church

The Disciples' Task

Jesus gave the Great Commission to His 11 disciples. Each were to go out to communicate his faith to another person, so they prayed, witnessed, and worked to win another person into the family of God. Then, each person they won was responsible to win someone else. But their strategy also involved planting churches with the confidence that every growing thing reproduces itself. So each church they planted would begin another church.

For 40 days of post-Resurrection ministry, Jesus taught His disciples the truths of the gospel and the new distinctives of the Church. Then came the 40th day, the last day He would physically be with His disciples. They forgot all about the Church and the new things. They had questions about the Old Testament.

"Lord, will You at this time restore the kingdom to Israel?" (Acts 1:6). When Jesus wanted them to look forward to the Church, they wanted to look back at the kingdom.

"It is not for you to know times or seasons which the Father has put in His own authority" (v. 7), Jesus responded. He knew their intentions were good, but there was a greater priority for them. Jesus would return, but while He was away, they had work to do.

"But you shall receive power when the Holy Spirit has come upon you; and you shall be witnesses to Me in Jerusalem, and in all Judea and Samaria, and to the end of the earth" (Acts 1:8).

"You shall be witnesses to Me" (v. 8). That was their commission in a nutshell. As they waited for the future Kingdom, they were to be His witnesses. The task would be to tell others what they had seen and heard and experienced. Jesus had already told them the Holy Spirit would work in the lives of unsaved people around them (John 16:7-11). Soon, the Holy Spirit would come upon them in a unique way.

Sometimes, the last thing a person says before he leaves is the most important thing to remember. As the disciples stood on the Mount of Olives that day, they must have realized they were experiencing a life-transforming moment. The thing Jesus was saying was really important. From this point on, they would use one word to define who they were. They were "witnesses."

The word "witness" is one of several terms in Scripture to describe the process we call *evangelism.* Evangelism is "communicating the gospel in an understandable manner and motivating the person to receive Christ and become a responsible member of His Church." Evangelism is perhaps the most exciting experience in which you will ever be involved. There is a sense of personal fulfillment and inner joy when you effectively share your faith with others that cannot be experienced any other way. God wants all of us involved in evangelism.

Various people picture different things when they think of an evangelist. For some, an evangelist is a famous preacher who travels from city to city "preaching the gospel." Others think of the host or hostess of a popular religious television program. Still others think of those brave church members who go door-to-door to talk to strangers about the gospel. Too often we define effective evangelism according to our stereotyped pictures of an evangelistic ministry. But the real key to effective evangelism is not found in a *program* but rather a *person,* the individual who would share his or her faith with others.

Evangelism is best captured in Jesus' use of the word *witness.* An effective witness has seen, heard, and experienced something; then he or she shares with others from that experience. The witness comes out of the overflow of his or her life. In that context, every Christian is a witness. Over the years, the authors have heard Christians use many excuses to explain why they can't witness. However noble these excuses may sound, they do not stand when examined in the context of Scripture.

At first glance, some of these excuses sound valid. You may have even thought of using them yourself at times. Fortunately, the Christians of the Early Church chose to ignore these excuses and witness anyway. The result of their faithful witness, and that of Christians in every generation since, is that we, too, have heard the gospel. And having heard the gospel, it is now entrusted to us to pass it on to our generation and those who follow us.

To make sure the world is evangelized, Jesus made us all witnesses, so no generation would ever be ignorant of "the wonderful works of God" (Acts 2:11). With such an important responsibility in our hands, we should do all we can to be a credible witness to those we meet.

Developing a Credible Witness

Those who are most effective in their witness of the Christian faith tend to be people who have developed a lifestyle that lends credibility to what they say. When they share their faith with others, it seems like the most natural thing for them to do. And those who hear them seem to be wanting to know more about how they, too, can experience a personal relationship with God.

What makes these people who witness for Christ so unique? Are they born this way, or can anyone learn to witness? If witnessing can be learned, is it possible to become a more effective witness? The Bible has much to say about the kind of person who is effective in evangelism. The good news is that it is possible for all Christians to develop a credible witness.

The most effective witness is one that flows out of a maturing Christian life. As we grow into a deeper relationship with God by dealing with problems in our lives, we will be more effective in sharing our faith with others (Ps. 51:10-13). People are going to be more responsive to the gospel when they see God working in your life than if you merely share abstract principles with others.

Part of the maturing process involves developing a genuine spiritual concern for others. This is called a burden that keeps us faithful in sharing our faith with others (Ps. 126:6). Certainly one of the keys to Paul's success in evangelism was his concern for those who did not know Christ as Savior (Rom. 9:1-3; 10:1).

Many Christians are effective in sharing their faith because they clearly understand the love of God (2 Cor. 5:14). People do things for love they would not do for any other reason, and they do it with more passion than they might otherwise. As we begin to realize just how much God loves us, we will find ourselves naturally sharing His love with others (1 John 4:9, 19: Rom. 5:5).

Perhaps it is our appreciation of God's love that gives us a servant's heart toward others. Because of Christ, we become willing to serve other people even when no one expects it (1 Cor. 9:19). Our willingness to help people adds to our credibility as we share the gospel (v. 22).

The effective witness believes in the power of the gospel to make a positive difference in others' lives (Rom. 1:16). When people come to faith in Jesus Christ, they become new creations (2 Cor. 5:17). The one who has personally experienced this change in his or her own life is more likely to recognize the life-changing potential of the gospel in the lives of others (1 Tim. 1:12-15).

People tend to listen to a witness when they have seen a positive difference in his or her lifestyle. This is especially true when they see the different way Christians respond to problems, because everyone struggles with trouble in this life. Peter reminded Christians to be prepared in the midst of their suffering to explain the gospel to those who ask (1 Pet. 3:14-17). He realized people would be attracted to Christianity when they saw the positive way Christians respond to problems. When unsaved family members see the consistent Christian witness of another in their home, they are often won to Christ even without someone explaining the gospel to them (v. 1).

Those most effective in evangelism tend to exercise wisdom in approaching people to discuss salvation (Dan. 12:3). They have acquired a special insight from God that makes them more effective in dealing with people (Prov. 11:30). But this insight is also available to all believers. When we recognize a need for greater wisdom in our own lives, we can get it by asking God (James 1:5). Also, when we make personal Bible study an ongoing spiritual discipline in our lives, we establish another means by which God provides us with His wisdom (Ps. 19:7).

Power for Witnessing

Because effective evangelism is done in the power of the Holy Spirit, the effective evangelist is one who has acquired unique spiritual power through the fullness of the Holy Spirit, that is, "Be filled with the Spirit" (Eph. 5:18). In the New Testament, the consistent evidence of the fullness of the Holy Spirit was spiritual power for evangelism (Acts 1:8). We can obtain this spiritual power by (1) wanting to be filled with the Holy Spirit, (2) repenting of known sin in our lives, (3) receiving the fullness of the Holy Spirit through prayer, and (4) trusting God to fill us and use us (John 7:37-39).

The same Holy Spirit who empowers us to be effective in evangelism also empowered the Scriptures to be effective in saving people (2 Tim. 3:15). One of the biblical expressions used to describe the Scriptures is "word of life" (Phil. 2:16), because the Bible is the Word of God that produces spiritual life in others. Many effective witnesses commit *Scripture to memory* to use when sharing the plan of salvation (Ps. 19:7). It is always easier to get a job done right when you have the right tools. In the work of evangelism, the Scriptures are the tools for witnessing.

There is something addictive about sharing the gospel

with others. As we begin sharing our faith with others, something happens to us internally. Wanting to tell others about Jesus can become the most natural response because we get an inner sense of fulfillment and joy. Before long, we find ourselves enjoying this ministry so much that we can barely conceive of not being involved in it (1 Cor. 9:16). What may seem so intimidating today can become a passionate part of our Christian life and ministry.

The Fullness of Power

When Jesus called His disciples and us to be witnesses, He knew He was calling us to something far beyond human ability. That is usually the way it is when we respond to God's call. The task is God-sized and really cannot be accomplished without God. That's why Jesus also promised His disciples they would receive spiritual power to enable them to witness effectively.

The Bible describes the power of God in the context of what that power has accomplished. First, there is the creative power of God that brought the world into existence (Jer. 10:12). Throughout the Old Testament, there are references to the military power of God that enabled Israel to triumph over its enemies (Exod. 15:6). Third, there is the resurrection power of God that raised Jesus from the dead (Phil. 3:10). Fourth, there is the victorious spiritual power of God that is able to defeat the devil (Rev. 12:10).

Appropriating the Power of God Personally

We live daily with some power at our disposal. We flip a switch on the wall for electric power. We turn the ignition key to have instant horsepower to drive our automobiles. In the home, school, or office, we are subject to powers of offices, organizations, and positions.

When the Bible describes power, two principles are emphasized. First, all "power belongs to God" (Ps. 62:11; Rom. 13:1). Second, "The God of Israel is He who gives strength and power to His people" (Ps. 68:35). There are several ways we can appropriate that power God is so eager to give us.

God gave a measure of His power to us when He saved us. The Scriptures repeatedly emphasize this truth. We are redeemed by power (Neh. 1:10) and have the privilege to call ourselves the children of God (John 1:12). Paul reminded the Ephesians that he was granted the gift of God's grace by His power (3:7). As Christians, we have access to the power of our Lord Jesus Christ (1 Cor. 5:4) and the spirit of power that God has given us (2 Tim. 1:7).

Although we have access to the power of God through our relationship with Christ, we can and should also pray for the power of God. When Paul prayed for the Thessalonians, he desired that God would give them power (2 Thess. 1:11). When we pray for spiritual power, there are several principles that should govern how we pray. First, God gives power to those who recognize their need (Isa. 40:29); therefore we should humbly acknowledge our need in prayer. Second, there is a relationship between power and faith (1 Pet. 1:5); therefore we should pray for power in faith. Third, there is an element of power closely tied to the name of Jesus (Acts 4:7-10); therefore we should claim power "in Jesus' name" (John 14:14). Fourth, when praying for power, we may be called upon to persevere and prevail in prayer (Gen. 32:28).

As we pray for spiritual power, God sometimes will bring to mind some weakness or sin in our lives that may be hindering our effectiveness in ministry. Jesus promised power to the one who overcame the corruption that had become part of church life in Thyatira (Rev. 2:26). The power that raised Jesus from the dead is related to the spirit of holiness (Rom. 1:4). A personal lifestyle of practical holiness will result in greater spiritual power. God wants each Christian to be clothed with holiness that is "the power of His might" (Eph. 6:10).

There is another dimension of spiritual power that is realized only as we are faithful in preaching the gospel. Paul identified the power of God in the gospel (Rom. 1:16), the preaching of the Cross (1 Cor. 1:18), and the Word of God itself (Heb. 4:12). When the people heard Jesus teaching the

Word of God during His public ministry, they also recognized an intrinsic power in those words (Luke 4:32).

Sometimes we fail to minister in the power of God because we fail to recognize and appreciate its presence. God wants us to celebrate His power already at work in our lives. In our worship of God, we should praise Him for His power (Ps. 21:13) and sing of His power at work in our lives (59:16). Many of the hymns are testimonial by nature and can be used to celebrate the power of God in our lives. As we worship God for who He is and what He is doing in our lives, we establish the environment in which He prefers to dwell (22:3). This suggests that worshiping God for His power may give us greater access to that power.

How to Be Filled with the Holy Spirit

Some Christians appear to serve God with greater effectiveness than others. This increased effectiveness cannot be explained by obvious factors such as education, personality, experience, or knowledge. Rather, they appear to have a spiritual power that energizes all they do for God.

Prior to His ascension, Jesus told His disciples to wait in Jerusalem until they were endued or clothed with the fullness of power (Luke 24:49). He knew they needed the power of God to achieve their full potential in the ministry of evangelism. He promised, "But you shall receive power when the Holy Spirit has come upon you" (Acts 1:8). The Acts of the Apostles records repeated accounts of the Early Church effectively reaching their world for Christ in the fullness of power.

Often zealous Christians attempt to do evangelism in their own strength rather than relying upon the power of God. While some limited success may be realized this way, doing evangelism in the fullness of the power of God results in greater evangelistic effectiveness. While some Christians may be satisfied with limited success in evangelism, those who want to be all God intended them to be will do what is necessary to acquire the fullness of power.

Paul commanded the Ephesians, "Be filled with the [Holy]

Spirit" (Eph. 5:18). God wants us to continually be filled or controlled by the Holy Spirit. The evidence of the fullness of the Holy Spirit in the Acts was the power of God manifested in bringing people to himself (1:8). On some occasions (but not every occasion) the building shook when Christians were filled with the Holy Spirit (4:31). But on every occasion, when Christians were filled with the Holy Spirit, the gospel was preached and people were saved.

On the final day of an observance of the Feast of Tabernacles, Jesus announced, "If anyone thirsts, let him come to Me and drink. He who believes in Me, as the Scripture has said, out of his heart will flow rivers of living water" (John 7:37-38). Jesus was referring to the fullness of the Holy Spirit when He made that statement (v. 39). In that statement, He identified the four steps we must take to experience the fullness of power associated with the Holy Spirit.

Being filled with the Holy Spirit begins with a thirst or deep desire to be filled. In His Sermon on the Mount, Jesus promised, "Blessed are those who hunger and thirst for righteousness, for they shall be filled" (Matt. 5:6). God will not fill a Christian with the Holy Spirit if he or she does not want to be filled.

Second, we must come to Jesus to be filled. Coming to Jesus involves first "coming from" or repenting of known sin in your life, and then "coming to" or yielding yourself to His complete control. Sin can hinder our relationship with God (Ps. 66:18), but "If we confess our sins, He is faithful and just to forgive us our sins and to cleanse us from all unrighteousness" (1 John 1:9). When we present ourselves completely to God, we "prove what is that good and acceptable and perfect will of God" (Rom. 12:1-2). God's will for our lives includes our being filled with the Holy Spirit (Eph. 5:17-18).

The third step in being filled involves drinking or receiving the gift God is offering. When we ask God for something that He has promised (Luke 11:13), we can be sure of receiving what we request. "Now this is the confidence that we have in Him, that if we ask anything according to His will,

He hears us. And if we know that He hears us, whatever we ask, we know that we have the petitions that we have asked of Him" (1 John 5:14-15).

The final step in being filled with the Holy Spirit involves believing, or taking God at His word (John 7:39). Paul asked the Galatians, "Did you receive the Spirit by the works of the law, or by the hearing of faith?" (3:2). The implied answer in that context is that they received the Holy Spirit by faith. "Without faith it is impossible to please Him [God]" (Heb. 11:6). We please God when we obey His command to be filled and believe His Word in the process.

The Pattern of an Effective Witness

When Jesus shared the Great Commission on this final occasion, He spoke of being a witness "in Jerusalem, and in all Judea and Samaria, and to the end of the earth" (Acts 1:8). Today, there are over 6 billion people on the planet. That is a lot of people to reach for Christ. If the task is ever to be accomplished in our generation, it needs to be done in a powerful way, but it also needs to be done in an organized way. If we don't, we will waste our limited resources and not have enough left to finish the task.

Many Bible teachers recognize a geographic pattern in the Great Commission. In this regard, Acts 1:8 is often viewed as the key verse in the history of the Early Church. It began in Jerusalem (chaps. 1—7), reached beyond into Judea and Samaria (chaps. 8—12), and then reached farther to the boundaries of the known world (chaps. 13—28). Your church may follow a similar evangelistic strategy by reaching its "Jerusalem," the area around the church, then starting daughter churches to reach beyond its immediate community ("Judea") and to ethnic groups within your community ("Samaria"). Then you pray that God might call some from these churches "to the end of the earth" as missionaries.

There may also be a theological pattern implied in the Great Commission. Jesus told His disciples to begin with those who had a historic contact with God (the Jews), move on to those less connected (Samaritans), and reach further to those with no contact at all (Gentiles). Paul seems to advocate this strategy when he describes the gospel as "the power of God to salvation for everyone who believes, for the Jew first and also for the Greek" (Rom. 1:16). As the apostles went to new towns to start churches, they looked for people most open to the gospel and began evangelizing them. Often they preached in the synagogues, but if the Jews opposed the message and Gentiles embraced it, the apostles worked with those most responsive.

The wonderful thing about God is that He loves the world. Since you are His, you must love all unconditionally. Love overcomes all barriers. If you love the people you are trying to reach, you will remove as many barriers as possible. You will reach out to them and draw them into your heart and into your fellowship. Remember in Christ, "There is neither Greek nor Jew, circumcised nor uncircumcised, barbarian, Scythian, slave nor free, but Christ is all and in all" (Col. 3:11).

Perhaps using the word "great" to describe the Great Commission is not such a bad idea after all. God has taken a "great" risk. We have been entrusted with a "great" message. We also face a "great" responsibility in taking the gospel to our world. But to partner with the Holy Spirit and witness in the fullness of God's power, what a "great" opportunity. And as others come to faith in Christ as a result of our witness, well, that would be "great!"

Personal Lessons to Take Away

1. I can share with others what I've seen, heard, and experienced in becoming a Christian.

2. I can rethink my objections to being a witness and simply share my faith with others.

3. I can experience the power of God in my life.

4. I can rely on the power of God when witnessing to other people.

5. I can be filled with the Spirit of God and thus experience the power of God.

Church Lessons to Take Away

1. Churches are planted by believers who witness about their faith to unsaved people in the area of the new church plant.

2. New churches are made up of believers who are won to Christ by those who intentionally witness for Christ.

3. Successful witnessing and church planting depends on the power of God working through those who are involved in a new church endeavor.

Personal Projects

Now it is time to put the Book of Acts into action. As you think about your task of evangelism or witnessing for Christ, choose one of the following projects this week to help you become more than a student of Scripture.

1. Are you onboard with what God is doing in our world today? He has left us here to be a witness. Consider the excuses you are inclined to use, saying you can't be a witness. Ask God to forgive you for not being a witness, and ask Him for the grace to overcome your excuse and obey Him anyway.

2. How credible is your witness for Christ? Remember, no matter how clean the water, people won't drink if it comes in dirty glasses. Review the section titled *Developing a Credible Witness*. As you read it, make a list of things you can do to improve the credibility factor in your witness. Don't allow a long list to get you discouraged. Instead, choose one area you will work on this week, and save the others for weeks to come. Even a small improvement will increase your credibility as a witness.

3. Are you still trying to witness for Jesus in your own strength? This job is too big for that. Review the sections on *Appropriating the Power of God Personally* and *How to Be Filled with the Holy Spirit*. What areas of the fullness of God's power have you failed to tap into? Make a list of things you could

do to appropriate the power of God in your life, and begin working on one of those disciplines this week. Next week, begin working on another. Take whatever time you need to become a more powerful witness for Christ.

Church Project

The apostles and women prepared themselves for Pentecost by praying in the Upper Room. Prayer was more than a meeting to them; it was absolutely important. If your church will successfully plant a new church, it must be founded in prayer. You must pray; all those on your church plant team must pray. Prayer is essential for success, will breathe life into your plans, is foundational for ministry, and will give power to all that is done.

Each team member must pray and then grow in prayer. They must grow in passion to pray, grow in ways to pray, grow in fellowship with God as they pray, and grow in getting bigger and bigger answers to prayer. Paul says, "Pray about everything" (Phil. 4:6, TLB) and "Pray all the time" (1 Thess. 5:17, TM). This project will help team members explore new fresh ways to pray, new territories, new prayer partners, and new priority areas.

1. *Start a prayer folder for the new church.* Use an 8½" x 11" file folder; it is the easiest to use and store. Put everything about the new church in this folder as a prayer reminder. Include flyers, announcements, letters, bulletin inserts, and so on. The items that get you excited about the new church will also motivate you to pray for each step of the project. Whether it's a community survey, talent search, or just passing out flyers, pray about each new step and each new event at the new church.

2. *Focus on personal and ministry-related readings.* Personal spiritual growth is paramount. How can you draw closer to Christ? What do you wish to read, Jonathan Edwards? David Brainerd? Zinzendorf, and others? (See Elmer Towns and Douglas Porter's book, *The Ten Greatest Revivals Ever,* to challenge you to God's work in ministry.)

3. *Make a list of personal spiritual goals.* God gives you a blank check in the area of spiritual growth; you must write in the amount. Growth in Bible knowledge is vital. Plan to read through the Bible each year. You can grow in prayer by writing down, dating, commenting on, and updating each answer. It will encourage you to continue on. God may not give us what we ask, but He will make us desire what He wants us to become and have.

> "The right way to pray is to write it all down."
> —John Arnold

4. *Find a foundational verse for church planting.* Choose a key verse or verses to be a basis for your prayer agenda (Matt. 16:18; 9:36-38).

5. *Pray for spiritual courage.* Most Christians are more than gun-shy when it comes to witnessing; they are shell-shocked. They need divine help and courage.

- Make a list of people you need to confront with the claims of Christ. Pray for them by name, and ask for courage to overcome inertia. Pray for an opportunity to witness to them.
- Make a list of others who need to be contacted and encouraged by you. Ask God to set up "His Divine Appointments." As you pray, find out if fear is selfishness.

6. *Church-related goals.* Pray that the church plant team be drawn together as a spiritual team. The best way is through seasons of prayer together (on their knees).

7. *Conclusion.* Leonard Ravenhill said in his book *Revival Praying,* "Most of us have enough grace to scrape through the day, but we have nothing over. We are conquerors but not 'more than conquerors.' We can fight off the enemy but we cannot take any prisoners. Ours is a defence action not an attacking power."

3

Saturating a Community with the Gospel

The Jerusalem Church

When Jesus ascended into heaven, the disciples returned to Jerusalem and met together with about 120 people to pray (see Acts 1). Things just didn't seem right without Jesus. While they knew something special was going to happen, there was a feeling that something was out of place. There were 12 tribes in Israel, and Jesus had called 12 apostles. But there were only 11 of them. Perhaps they feared their ministry would not emerge until "the Eleven" once more became "the Twelve."

Peter rose to remind them that the betrayal of Judas Iscariot was consistent with the prophecies that the Messiah would be betrayed. He was not trying to justify the actions of the betrayer but rather recognized that his sin should not surprise them. Peter cited two psalms (69:25; 109:8) as a basis to appoint a new 12th disciple.

Several conditions were quickly established to appoint a disciple to replace Judas Iscariot. First, the new disciple would have traveled with Jesus from the beginning (after John the Baptist baptized Jesus). Second, the new disciple should have been a witness of both the resurrection and ascension of Jesus. Of those present, only two appeared to meet all these qualifications: Joseph Justus, who was also known as Barsabas, and Matthias.

With two equally qualified candidates for one office, the disciples were not prepared to make a decision themselves without some sort of divine guidance. Together they prayed, "You, O Lord, who know the hearts of all, show which of these two You have chosen to take part in this ministry and apostleship from which Judas by transgression fell" (Acts 1:24-25). Then, relying upon the Old Testament custom of casting lots, they determined Matthias was the one who should serve in Judas Iscariot's place. "And he was numbered with the eleven apostles" (v. 26).

During the nearly two weeks of corporate prayer that took place between the ascension of Jesus and the Day of Pentecost, there were times of inner searching, confession, worship, and intercession. Various reconciliations would have had to have been made in a group of that size. By the end of the waiting period, a spirit of unity governed the group as "they were all with one accord in one place" (2:1).

A Church Born in a Revival

Quite unexpectedly, a number of strange phenomena began to take place in and around the Upper Room. First, there was a sound of a strong gust of wind that seemed to echo from the walls of the room where they were sitting. Then divided tongues that looked like flames of a fire began appearing on each of them. Third, "they were all filled with the Holy Spirit" (2:4), an experience that had previously happened on only rare occasions in the Old Testament, and almost never in a group setting. Then each of them began to speak clearly in foreign languages they had never learned. All this happened very early on the Day of Pentecost, before 9:00 in the morning.

Because Jewish males were required by the Law of Moses to attend the feast (Deut. 16:16), the city was crowded with pious Jewish men from around the Roman Empire who had come to celebrate Pentecost. News of what had taken place in the Upper Room quickly spread through the crowded city. As a crowd began to form around the disciples, the people were divided as to just what happened. At least 16 different language groups heard these Galileans speaking fluently in their native tongue. Others, probably unable to understand the different languages they heard, simply assumed the group was drunk on new wine.

Peter stood in the middle of the group to explain it was too early for anyone to be drunk, but rather they were witnessing an outpouring of the Holy Spirit, as prophesied by the prophet Joel (Acts 2:16-21; Joel 2:18-32). Apparently, the message Peter announced to the multitude was repeated by different disciples in the new languages they were now speaking so everyone could understand what Peter was saying. While not all the specific details of Joel's prophecy were fulfilled on the Day of Pentecost, enough were present to confirm that the crowd was witnessing something similar to that outpouring of the Spirit of which Joel and other prophets wrote. Many Bible teachers believe that the ultimate outpouring will take place at the second coming of Christ.

Definition of Revival
God pouring out His presence on His people

The outpouring of the Holy Spirit has been largely ignored by Christians throughout the centuries, except during times of evangelical revival in the Church. While the Holy Spirit is a person, the Scriptures sometimes portray Him as being "poured out" like water upon thirsty people in need of God's blessing. It marks a period of spiritual intensity in which the presence of the Holy Spirit is recognized by others and His work of revival is experienced by Christians. An outpouring of the Holy Spirit is most often accompanied by an awakening of the unsaved to their need for salvation and an eventual reformation of the society in which the outpouring takes place.

When Peter said, "This is what was spoken by the prophet Joel" (Acts 2:16), he was describing the revival in Jerusalem as a prototype of revival in this age. While many Christians claim they would like to experience revival in their church and community, most are convinced revival will not likely come. But revival is one of the ways God energizes a church to effectively reach its community. Revival can come to any church if they are prepared to meet the conditions God has tied to an outpouring of the Holy Spirit. Ironically, many of the reasons people believe their church could never experience revival are really indicators God is ready to do something special in their midst.

The Message of a Revived Church

As Peter explained the signs of that day in the context of the outpouring of the Holy Spirit, he pointed to an even greater sign that had taken place just seven weeks earlier. "Jesus of Nazareth, a Man attested by God to you by miracles, wonders, and signs which God did through Him in your midst, as you yourselves also know—Him being delivered by the determined purpose and foreknowledge of God, you have taken by lawless hands, have crucified, and put to death; whom God raised up, having loosed the pains of death, because it was not possible that He should be held by it" (Acts 2:22-24).

Peter explained the meaning of the Old Testament as Jesus had explained it to him. He also explained the meaning of the Crucifixion and Resurrection in the context of two familiar messianic psalms (16:8-11; 110:1). Just as Peter and the other disciples had not understood the real significance of these psalms until after Jesus opened their understanding (see Luke 24:25), so many of those who heard Peter preach on Pentecost had never before thought of the Messiah as One who would suffer and be raised from the dead. Peter explained these psalms could not logically be applied to David who first penned these words because the corrupted remains of David's body were still in David's tomb. He concluded the prophecy must be applied to Jesus who rose from the dead. That made Jesus unique. He concluded, "Therefore let all the house of Israel know assuredly that God has made this Jesus, whom you crucified, both Lord and Christ" (Acts 2:36).

Many who heard Peter's logical explanation of what was

taking place were deeply convicted of their sin. The Greek verb *katenugēsan,* which is translated "to cut" (v. 37), was a term used by classical writers to report the devastation of a city by an invading army. Peter's words had brought about a conviction so severe that the people stood devastated in their heart before God. Desperately, they wanted to do something to appease the inevitable wrath of God. "Men and brethren," they cried out, "what shall we do?" (v. 37).

Peter called them to repent from their sin and trust Jesus as their Messiah. The outward evidence of such an inner response to the gospel would be submitting to what has become known as Christian baptism. "Let everyone of you be baptized in the name of Jesus Christ for the remission of sins; and you shall receive the gift of the Holy Spirit" (v. 38). Then Peter seemed to indicate the outpouring of the Spirit being experienced that day would not be limited to that day or city. "For the promise is to you and to your children, and to all who are afar off, as many as the Lord our God will call" (v. 39).

That day, about 3,000 people eagerly responded to Peter's message and were baptized, adding to the infant Church in Jerusalem. Because of the Jews' tendency to send only the head of the household to Jerusalem during the feasts, most likely the Church was a predominantly male institution in its early days. Many of those who responded may have been in town only for the feast and within days or weeks left Jerusalem to carry the message of the gospel back to their hometowns and cities. Those converted would spread the gospel in other parts of Judea and to the known world.

Reaching Out to Others

Those who made decisions to identify with Christ and His Church were deeply committed. "They continued steadfastly in the apostles' doctrine and fellowship, and in the breaking of bread, and in prayers" (Acts 2:42). A spirit of community quickly developed to the point that they freely shared their possessions with others in the group. Because of the size of the group, there were few places where they could meet together.

They met daily in the Temple as a larger group celebrating their newly found faith, but also met in smaller groups in homes throughout the city to nurture the fellowship that had developed within the group. Others, who were not converted on Pentecost, were saved later, "and the Lord added to the church daily those who were being saved" (v. 47).

The evangelistic outreach on the Day of Pentecost was not the only example of mass evangelism. A little later, about 3:00 one afternoon, Peter and John were unexpectedly involved in another large evangelistic outreach. They were on their way to the Temple to pray when they were approached by a lame beggar, begging for alms at the gate of the Temple. Neither of the disciples had funds to give the beggar, but that did not stop Peter from addressing him. Once he had the beggar's attention, Peter explained, "Silver and gold I do not have, but what I do have I give you: In the name of Jesus Christ of Nazareth, rise up and walk" (Acts 3:6). Then Peter took the beggar by the hand and began to lift him to his feet.

Suddenly the beggar felt strength returning to the bones in his ankles and feet. He not only stood but also jumped and walked around the Temple with the two apostles, praising God. In his enthusiasm, his worship of God soon attracted a crowd. This beggar was well known at the gate of the Temple, and those who gathered around wondered what had happened to enable him to stand in the Temple. Peter soon perceived that some in the crowd were beginning to conclude he had a special power that resulted in this amazing miracle. Eager to set the record straight, Peter stood in Solomon's Porch and used the occasion to once again preach the gospel.

The focus of his message was the crucifixion and resurrection of Christ. Peter pulled no punches in clearly affixing the blame for Jesus' death on them. After reminding his listeners that Pilate had attempted to release Jesus, Peter noted, "But you denied the Holy One and the Just, and asked for a murderer to be granted to you, and killed the Prince of life, whom God raised from the dead, of which we are witnesses" (vv. 14-15). As in his previous sermon, Peter again called on those who heard him to repent and "be converted, that your sins may be blotted out" (v. 19). Many who heard him believed in Christ for salvation. By the end of the day, about 5,000 men were actively involved with the church at Jerusalem (4:4).

When the Going Got Tough

There was also another response to Peter's preaching. The apostle attracted the attention of the priests and Sadducees. The Pharisees had been in control of the Sanhedrin when Jesus was crucified, but it was perceived they botched the job, so the Sadducees had assumed control. They tended to deny the supernatural in their concept of religion and were "greatly disturbed that they taught the people and preached in Jesus the resurrection from the dead" (4:2). Had Peter avoided references to the Resurrection in his message, he and John probably would not have been arrested. But the gospel without the Resurrection is not the gospel, and the two apostles and the man who had been healed were taken into custody and spent the night in jail.

The next day, the high priests and other leading Jewish leaders met to discuss the matter. They brought the three men before them to inquire concerning the source of their miraculous power to heal the lame. Peter wasted no time getting directly to the heart of the gospel. "Let it be known to you all, and to all the people of Israel, that by the name of Jesus Christ of Nazareth, whom you crucified, whom God raised from the dead, by Him this man stands here before you whole" (v. 10). He went on to stress that salvation could only be found in the name of that same Jesus (v. 12).

Those who heard the apostles speak that day were perplexed. Without a doubt, these men were fishermen and had no formal theological education. It was also obvious "that they had been with Jesus" (v. 13). When they were dismissed from the room in which the hearing was being conducted, the Sanhedrin began discussing their options. Obviously, a significant miracle had occurred that could not reasonably be denied. They decided their best hope was to convince the

apostles not to talk to others about Jesus. When they pro-
nounced their sentence, the apostles would not agree to it.
"Whether it is right in the sight of God to listen to you more
than to God, you judge. For we cannot but speak the things
which we have seen and heard" (vv. 19-20). The council
threatened them further but eventually released the apostles
without punishing them. They realized the miracle had
broad popular support and chose not to alienate the people
by punishing the ones through whom the miracle was accomplished.

When they were released, Peter and John reported to the
Church all that had taken place. When the Christians heard
what had taken place, they all prayed for boldness to continue to be faithful in proclaiming the message: "Now, Lord,
look on their threats, and grant to Your servants that with all
boldness they may speak Your word" (v. 29).

God granted their request. "And when they had prayed,
the place where they were assembled together was shaken;
and they were all filled with the Holy Spirit, and they spoke
the word of God with boldness" (v. 31).

In the face of opposition, the quality of their fellowship
continued to grow along with their numbers. "Now the multitude of those who believed were of one heart and one soul;
neither did anyone say that any of the things he possessed
was his own, but they had all things in common" (v. 32). In
one example of corporate sharing, a converted Levite named
Joses earned the nickname Barnabas, meaning "Son of Encouragement," and sold his real estate holdings in Cyprus to
meet the needs of others.

As the Church continued to grow, its ministry expanded,
touching more lives than before. The ministry reached beyond Jerusalem to the surrounding cities. Yet with the success
of the ministry, they were once again attacked by the Sadducees. The apostles were arrested and put in prison. During
the evening, they were released by an angel. When the officers arrived the next morning, they found the prison shut up
and well guarded, but no prisoners were inside. While the

leading priests attempted to understand what was going on, they received a report claiming, "The men whom you put in prison are standing in the temple and teaching the people!" (Acts 5:25).

The officers were sent to arrest them. When the apostles were brought before the council, they were immediately accused. "Did we not strictly command you not to teach in this name? And look, you have filled Jerusalem with your doctrine, and intend to bring this Man's blood on us!" (v. 28). But the apostles were not intimidated by the council. "We ought to obey God rather than men," they affirmed (v. 29). Then once again they reminded the Sanhedrin of the essence of their message. "The God of our fathers raised up Jesus whom you murdered by hanging on a tree" (v. 30).

Saturation Evangelism

Although the expression had not yet been coined, the Church in Jerusalem practiced what has been called "saturation evangelism." Saturation evangelism involves preaching the gospel to every available person, at every available time, by every available means. This definition comes from "filling Jerusalem" with the gospel. Saturation evangelism is successful because it contacts people where they are, keeps on contacting people, and never stops contacting people. Churches that practice saturation evangelism make winning people for Christ a passion.

The message of saturation evangelism is the gospel. Paul later summarized the message of the gospel when he wrote, "Christ died for our sins according to the Scriptures, and that He was buried, and that He rose again the third day according to the Scriptures" (1 Cor. 15:3-4). When a church practices saturation evangelism, their message consistently points people to the Savior.

The target of saturation evangelism is people. An evangelist once expressed frustration after conducting an evangelistic meeting where the host church did everything except insure unsaved people were present. When a church practices saturation evangelism, people are the focus, not programs. Church programs are designed to reach people. If they are ineffective in accomplishing that purpose, change them to become more effective or replace them with a new and effective way to reach people.

The force of saturation evangelism is found in touching the lost in your community. Evangelism is not limited to a Tuesday evening visitation team or Saturday morning outreach effort. Saturation evangelism makes sharing the gospel a priority every hour of every day. Churches using this strategy must look to the example of the church at Jerusalem: "Daily in the temple, and in every house, they did not cease teaching and preaching Jesus as the Christ" (Acts 5:42).

The strategy of saturation evangelism is varied. Whereas many evangelistic churches use one or two effective evangelism strategies, churches that practice saturation evangelism are always looking for new ways to reach people for Christ. They design church ads to reach people and widely distribute gospel literature to tell the story of Jesus. Keep the name of your church constantly before the public. Look for ways to use the local media to saturate your town with your message, using radio, television, and the print media simultaneously.

Getting Too Big to Quit

Evangelical churches believe in the importance of reaching people for Christ, but not all consistently practice evangelism. Evangelism involves communicating the gospel in the power of the Holy Spirit to unconverted people with the intent of effecting conversions. When a church builds its ministry around the Great Commission, those who repent of their sin and trust Christ as Savior are encouraged to serve the Lord as part of the fellowship of that local church. New believers become part of the team to reach others for Christ.

Even some churches that actually practice evangelism do so for the wrong reason. A small church struggling to make ends meet may be convinced by their pastor to reach out to the community to help them keep the church open. When the church grows and has enough workers and money to maintain their status quo, their commitment to reaching others may wane. But Jesus never gave the Great Commission to make church comfortable, or to just keep it going.

The story of the Church at Jerusalem reveals there are no practical limits to church size and there are no limits to evangelism. By the end of the Day of Pentecost, there were 3,000 involved in the Church. In the early days, "the Lord added to the church daily" (Acts 2:47). Very soon that number grew to 5,000. Before long, "the number of the disciples was multiplying" (6:1). Notice the change in the arithmetic terms from adding to multiplying. According to the historical records of the time, it is estimated that eventually about half of the 200,000 people then living in Jerusalem were converted to Christ and added to that Church.

A small church in a community may close its doors and cease its ministry virtually unnoticed, but as a church begins reaching people and growing, it will become too big to quit the work of saturation evangelism. The light that shines farthest shines brightest at home. Jesus told His disciples, "The field is the world" (Matt. 13:38). Even if a church managed to reach 100 percent of the people living in their community, they have still not saturated the world with the gospel. Jesus also said, "Let us go into the next towns, that I may preach there also, because for this purpose I have come forth" (Mark 1:38).

Even as the Church in Jerusalem grew, it reached out beyond its city limits. "Also a multitude gathered from the surrounding cities to Jerusalem, bringing sick people and those who were tormented by unclean spirits, and they were all healed" (Acts 5:16). The Church at Jerusalem may have been establishing new churches in area cities even before the persecution intensified. It is clear that the practice of evangelizing area towns intensified when the persecution forced many to flee to other cities to escape the persecution (8:1, 4).

Personal Lessons to Take Away

1. I can pray for the success of a new church.

2. I can be part of saturating a new community with the gospel so that a new church can be planted.

3. I should expect opposition to me personally and to my church when the gospel is successfully planted and the new church begins to grow.

4. I should pray and expect revival that is associated with a new church plant.

5. I can accomplish more for God when I minister in the power of the Holy Spirit.

6. I should expect a successful church plant to reach out to other surrounding areas in evangelism and ministry, even beginning other new churches.

Church Lessons to Take Away

1. New churches best establish their ministry by a strong presentation of the gospel.

2. New churches can be successfully planted by communicating the gospel to every available person in the new area of outreach, at every available time, by every available means.

3. New churches grow when they are begun in an environment of revival when God pours His Spirit on the new ministry.
   a. New churches should expect opposition, because Satan and evil men are opposed to a message of holiness, repentance, and accountability to God.
   b. Before beginning a new church, there should be a concerted season of fasting and prayer for the blessing of God on the new endeavor.
   c. New churches should reach out into surrounding areas to evangelize other areas with the gospel, perhaps even plant another church.

Personal Projects

Though they were novices, the Christians in Jerusalem seemed to get it right. Energized by revival and committed to the Great Commission, they managed to saturate their community with the gospel despite intense opposition by influential people. They even managed to reach out beyond their community to start new churches throughout Judea. Now it is our turn to put the Book of Acts back into action.

1. Throughout history, God has used revival to energize churches to reach their community and world for Christ. Is there something in your life that might hinder the coming of revival to your church? Compare your attitudes and activities with the kinds of things God looks for when He sends revival.

2. One of the marks of the first Christians was that they were sensitive to opportunities to share the gospel with those they met. That may be one reason why the Lord added to their church "daily." What did you do last week to reach people? As you look back over the last week, were there opportunities you failed to recognize or utilize to share the gospel? How will things be different this week? As you reflect on the faithful witness of the early Christians saturating their community with the gospel in good times and bad, ask God to open your eyes to opportunities He provides and give you the grace to use them this week.

3. The church at Jerusalem understood the Great Commission was not intended as just a tool for church growth but as the mission of the Church itself. Has your church reached its comfort zone or gotten too big? Review the section *Getting Too Big to Quit,* and begin thinking about new neighborhoods or nearby communities where your church could begin a new church. Ask God to impress on you a particular area; then share your concerns with your Bible study group leader and pastor. If several of you are impressed with the same community, God may want your church to begin a new church in that area.

Church Project

1. Planning saturation evangelism. Your ministry team should make plans to saturate the new area with the gospel, even as new plans are formulated for planting a church:

- Appoint an advertising leader and team.
- Make plans to use some of the following: radio, TV, newspaper, web sites, press releases, ads in shoppers' magazines, cable TV, posters, flyers, directional signs to new church property, visitation, get acquainted meetings, and so forth.
- Begin making a calendar to "saturate" the new areas. The calendar will assign dates when each form of advertising will be used. The calendar will need to be correlated with other actual events in church planting.

2. Planning for revival:

- Actually, no one can predict when revival will come. However, God's people can meet the requirements that bring revival: "If my people, which are called by my name, shall humble themselves, and pray, and seek my face, and turn from their wicked ways; then will I hear from heaven, and will forgive their sin, and will heal their land" (2 Chron. 7:14, KJV).
- Call prayer meetings to pray for revival.
- Teach the ministry team the conditions necessary to bring a revival.

3. Plan for concerted prayer immediately before a church plant:

- *There is power in the volume of people prayer.*
  Make plans to involve as many people in prayer as possible: for example, prayer meetings at the sending church and home prayer meetings in new areas; establish a prayer clock schedule (get 24 people to pray for the church plant, one person assigned to each hour of the day, praying for two weeks before the church launch); get a number of people to pray one hour a day, a week, a month for the new church plant (Matt. 26:40).
- *There is value in the volume of time spent in prayer.*
  Make plans to get prayer from other churches in the denomination, others in the sending church, friends of members of the ministry team, other Christians in the area.

4

A Layperson Helping to Plant a Church

The Church in Samaria

Persecution on the new Church in Jerusalem was growing. In addition, inside the Church there were different problems. The explosive growth made it difficult to keep up with details of ministry. The apostles couldn't adequately supervise everything. They knew they had to give priority to prayer and the preaching of the gospel. It is not surprising that before long, an internal dissension began to develop in the Church.

While the Church at Jerusalem was predominantly Jewish in character, it had two different ethnic groups, Palestinian Jews and Hellenistic Jews. The Palestinian Jews tended to adhere to the Old Testament law on things like food and social customs, whereas the Hellenistic Jews were more liberal. They had adopted aspects of Gentile culture into their lifestyle. The normal ethnic tensions between these two groups soon erupted in the new Church. The Hellenistic Jews began complaining their widows were being overlooked as food and other supplies were being distributed.

The Hellenistic Jews had a valid point, but the apostles did not have the time to personally distribute relief without abandoning their primary task of prayer and preaching. When the murmuring came to the attention of the apostles, they recognized the severe impact this minor problem could have if it was not solved. Therefore, the apostles concluded,

"It is not desirable that we should leave the word of God and serve tables" (Acts 6:2). The apostles proposed the Church select seven men who could be appointed to supervise the distribution to the widows. While the term "deacon" is not used to describe these men in this context, many Bible teachers look at these seven men as the first deacons of the Church. In this context, the apostle stressed four essential qualities of these first church officers: (1) a good reputation, (2) full of the Holy Spirit, (3) full of wisdom, (4) full of faith (vv. 3, 5).

The Church agreed with the wisdom of the apostles and selected seven men. It is interesting to note that each of these men have Greek names and therefore probably had a Hellenistic background. One of the seven is specifically identified as "a proselyte from Antioch" (v. 5). This would make Nicolas the first Gentile church officer. This meant the new Church bent over backward to be fair.

Prayers were then offered to induct these new servants into ministry. As a result of this action, a problem that threatened the Church resulted in strengthening the Church. "And the word of God spread, and the number of disciples multiplied greatly in Jerusalem, and a great many of the priests were obedient to the faith" (v. 7). The priests who opposed the Christian message because of its focus on the resurrection of Jesus embraced the gospel when they realized how the Christian message had changed lives and resolved problems, especially money problems.

Can God Use Laypeople in Ministry?

As the newly converted priests became part of the life of the Early Church, they must have found the Church's emphasis on lay ministry somewhat strange. All priests were physical descendants of Aaron, Israel's first high priest. From the moment they were born, they were prepared for a career involved in some aspect of Temple worship. As a son learned his trade from his father, so the son of a priest learned how to be a priest by observing his father. Like other small boys in the community, he attended the local synagogue school. When he got older, he attended one of several recognized schools that trained him in various skills priests were expected to have. At age 30, he began his active service as a priest.

Christianity differed from Judaism in its view of ministry. Jesus himself was from the tribe of Judah and, therefore, would have been considered unqualified to be one of the priests. He was accepted to teach the law as a rabbi, but His birth disqualified Him as a priest. The priest would have considered Jesus a lay teacher. When He called disciples, they likewise became lay teachers. Most had developed a business interest long before they followed Jesus. They, too, were viewed suspiciously by the religious establishment because they preached without first being trained in a recognized rabbinical school (Acts 4:13).

The appointment of seven laymen from the congregation to assist in ministry was a statement that laypeople would be part of ministry in the new Church. It is likely many of the 120 in the Upper Room were laypeople who had been involved in ministry on the Day of Pentecost. Also, another reason the Lord may have added to the Church daily was that the people were daily witnessing to their friends. When the apostles gathered the congregation to choose seven men, they were initiating the widespread practice of using laypersons in ministry. This became an official policy of the Church.

Despite the commitment of the apostles to lay ministry, this approach has not always been followed throughout history. As various denominations developed schools to train ministers, those ministers often served alongside laypeople in their churches. Before long, many laypeople realized they were not as well trained as their pastors. Because their pastor did not train them to be more effective in ministry, many laypeople withdrew from ministry and left it to the professionals. As more and more of the laity dropped out, the view that laypeople are not needed in ministry became more widely believed.

Throughout history, churches that have developed a clergy approach to ministry have usually become ingrown and ultimately are not able to significantly impact society. In contrast, churches that have emphasized the importance of lay involvement have had a profound impact on their culture.

Some of America's largest church denominations are the result of widespread lay ministry within their churches.

The existence of Methodist and other Holiness denominations across America is to a large extent due to the commitment of men like John Wesley and Francis Asbury to use lay ministry. Wesley himself was trained as an Anglican clergyman, but as the Evangelical Revival began spreading in England, he quickly recognized he would not have ordained clergy to help him. Wesley and others preached widely and often, but the demand for Methodist preachers was greater than they could meet. The Methodists appointed laymen as circuit riding preachers, and with only a few sermons to preach, they gathered people together in churches. Francis Asbury, first leader of Methodism in the United States, emphasized lay ministry, and his strategy was adopted by various other Holiness denominations.

The largest denomination in America also owes its success to its historic emphasis on lay ministry. Traditionally, Baptist pastors trained their people in various aspects of ministry and encouraged laymen who felt "called to preach" to do so even without formal theological education. In Britain, Charles Spurgeon began preaching when he was only 16, and eventually built the largest known church in the world, that is, the Metropolitan Tabernacle. His only ministerial training came from watching his grandfather preach. Spurgeon devoted much of his ministry to training "ploughboy preachers" to be effective in ministry. When Southern Baptists in America focused on using laypeople to build great Sunday Schools, they built the largest denomination in the nation. Many who learned to teach the Bible as Sunday School teachers became lay preachers in extension ministries, thus helping plant new Baptist churches.

More recently, various Pentecostal denominations have experienced significant growth worldwide by the widespread use of laypeople in ministry. Many of the pastors of large Pentecostal churches, especially in the emerging world, have never attended a theological seminary. In most cases, their ministry grew out of their personal witness as a layperson. When it became too big for them to do while maintaining a secular job, they began drawing a salary from the church. As they grew in ministry, they attended conferences and read books to learn more and became more effective.

Originally in the Old Testament, God wanted everyone in ministry. He wanted Israel to become "a kingdom of priests and a holy nation" (Exod. 19:6). In the New Testament, Peter uses that same language to describe the Church (1 Pet. 2:9). The examples of two laymen of the seven demonstrate how laypeople can become involved in ministry today.

The Ministry of Stephen

Stephen is the first of the seven described in detail. Even though he was involved with new responsibilities in caring for the widows, he also had other ministry opportunities. Stephen was an able communicator and often disputed in Hellenistic synagogues in Jerusalem including the Synagogue of the Freedmen. Rabbis and rabbinical students from Asia who came to Jerusalem to study the law probably attended that synagogue. Many Bible teachers believe that may have also been the synagogue where Saul of Tarsus attended when he was in Jerusalem.

It was not unusual in the synagogues to allow a visitor to teach and then debate their message if it was contrary to what they believed. As a result, the synagogue was always a place of lively discussion. Leading teachers in the synagogue would typically challenge what was viewed as doctrinal error and show the superiority of their own view. But when Stephen preached the gospel in this synagogue, "they were not able to resist the wisdom and the Spirit by which he spoke" (Acts 6:10).

Because they could not defeat Stephen through the normally effective means of debate in the synagogue, several of the more prominent members of that synagogue secretly arranged to have men report that Stephen was guilty of blasphemy. This was a serious charge and was effective in inciting the people and Jewish leaders against Stephen. He was seized and brought before the council. There, false witnesses accused, "This man does not cease to speak blasphemous words against this holy place and the law; for we have heard him say that this Jesus of Nazareth will destroy this place and change the customs which Moses delivered to us" (vv. 13-14).

After the witnesses were heard, the whole council focused their attention on Stephen as he presented his defense. Stephen began to build his argument by reviewing the history of Israel. Like the apostles before him, he charged the council with having rejected Christ. His words brought deep conviction to the hearts of the Sanhedrin, just as Peter's words on Pentecost had brought similar conviction. But rather than looking for a way to get right with God, the council turned on Stephen with anger. As he continued to speak, "they cried out with a loud voice, stopped their ears, and ran at him with one accord; and they cast him out of the city and stoned him" (7:57-58).

One of those present that day was a young promising Pharisee named Saul of Tarsus. Later, he claimed when the balloting was taken to sentence Stephen, "I cast my vote against [him]" (26:10). As others actually stoned Stephen, Saul watched over their coats. Although not on the front line, he must have heard the dying Stephen pray his final words, "Lord, do not charge them with this sin" (7:60).

In his career as a Pharisee and member of the Sanhedrin, Saul had probably witnessed several executions, but he had not seen many men die like Stephen. He was probably more accustomed to hearing hardened criminals curse God and the Romans. Many Bible teachers believe Stephen's preaching and death planted a seed that would later produce fruit on the Damascus road in the conversion of Paul.

Finding a Ministry in Your Community

Just as Stephen found a place to minister in his community, you can find a place to minister within your community. In most churches, there are always more things to be done than there are people to do them. Often, churches attempt to compensate by having their best workers take on several jobs. While that might help on a temporary basis, long term it produces burned-out workers and perhaps a greater shortage.

As you look for a ministry in your church, you might want to begin as an apprentice. Throughout history, the way one learned a trade was to assist a master of that trade. Before teaching a Sunday School class or leading your own Bible study group in a home, you might want to work with those who are already doing it and learn from their example. Most teachers would appreciate the help and opportunity to multiply their ministry by training others. As you become more comfortable with the ministry you learn as an apprentice, you may also become the key to continued growth in your church.

Some churches provide specialized training for various ministries in the church, perhaps an entry-level seminar to help people find the best ministry fit for them. If there is a particular ministry in your church that interests you, you may want to talk with that ministry leader to find opportunities to serve. That conversation could be the beginning of a significant and rewarding ministry experience.

Sometimes God gives laypeople a special burden for ministry that doesn't fit into the existing ministry of a local church. Perhaps God wants you to launch a new ministry in your church to meet a neglected or overlooked need. It may be that God has given a similar burden to several people who can work together as a new ministry team in your church. If God has given you a burden for a new ministry in your church, discuss your idea with your pastor or other church leaders responsible for similar ministries. Remember, you are now a part of a church that once was considered a "new ministry" project.

The Ministry of Philip

Following the death of Stephen, the persecution of the Church intensified. Because the Sanhedrin was based in Jerusalem, the persecution in the city was more intense than in the outlying communities. As people began to recognize this, many moved to other communities throughout Judea. Some moved beyond Judea into other regions far from Jerusalem. As they left, they took their Christian faith to new communities that had not yet heard the gospel.

> *"As for Saul, he made havoc of the church, entering every house, and dragging off men and women, committing them to prison"* (Acts 8:3-4).

Samaria was one of the most unlikely places a Jewish leader would pursue fleeing Christians. This may have been one reason Philip and others chose Samaria as their new home. When Philip arrived in "the city of Samaria" (probably Shechem), he "preached Christ to them" (8:5). These people had been exposed earlier to the ministry by both John the Baptist and Jesus. It is not surprising, therefore, that the Samaritans were receptive to the gospel as they heard it from Philip.

Philip's preaching was also confirmed by various authenticating signs. Unclean spirits were cast out of the possessed, and many lame and with forms of paralysis were miraculously healed. As more people turned to Christ, they experienced the benefits of these miracles and "there was great joy in that city" (v. 8).

Among those converted in Philip's ministry was a former sorcerer named Simon. He had a reputation because of his ability to make incantations or perform other aspects of occult ritual. But when Philip began performing miracles in Samaria, Simon readily confessed, "This man is the great power of God" (v. 10). Simon himself converted to Christianity and was baptized by Philip. The conversion of Simon influenced many in the city to reconsider Philip's message, and they, too, came to faith in Christ.

Philip's ministry in Samaria was consistent with the intent of the Great Commission to be witnesses "in . . . Samaria" (1:8). As news of the new church reached Jerusalem, the apostles visited the city to confirm the new ministry. Philip's ministry among the Samaritans marked a new territory for Christianity. When Peter and John left the Samaritan church to begin their journey back to Jerusalem, they traveled more slowly than they may have normally, "preaching the gospel in many villages of the Samaritans" (8:25).

As significant as Philip's ministry was in Samaria, God had something else in store for him to do. God sent Philip to travel "south along the road which goes down from Jerusalem to Gaza" (v. 26). It was only when he arrived that Philip learned the reason for his journey. There he met a prominent Ethiopian official in the government of Queen Candace of Ethiopia. The Ethiopian had probably traveled to Jerusalem on a religious pilgrimage but left the city with more questions than answers. When Philip found the man reading the scroll of Isaiah, he used the opportunity to explain the gospel to the man. Before long, the Ethiopian trusted Christ as Savior and was baptized. According to an early tradition of the Ethiopian Coptic Church, this man then carried the gospel back to his native land and established that church.

After baptizing the Ethiopian and perhaps others in his company, Philip was taken by the Holy Spirit west to the city of Azotus, near the Mediterranean Sea. Philip continued his ministry of preaching from town to town, working up the coast until he came to the city of Caesarea. There he apparently settled with his family, although he never abandoned his commitment to sharing the gospel with others. Beginning his lifetime of ministry as a layman, Philip became the only individual in the New Testament called an evangelist (21:8).

Finding a Community for Your Ministry

Just as Philip looked outside his community for ministry, you may want to look for ministry opportunities in another community. Perhaps God wants you to be part of the ministry team that will launch a new church in a nearby community.

While there are many ways to start new churches, one method, which has been widely used, involves your home church commissioning some of its leaders and people to begin a new church in another part of town or neighboring community. This is sometimes called the mother-daughter approach to church planting. The existing church is the mother church that gives birth to a new church, the daughter church.

One of the difficulties faced in church planting is the lack of mature leadership in a new church. An effective evangelistic pastor may lead many people to Christ in a new church, but his converts lack the spiritual maturity to assume critical leadership roles. The mother-daughter approach to church planting alleviates this problem by giving a new church a more complete ministry team. Churches committed to starting daughter churches will train leaders and encourage them to use their gifts as part of the new church planting effort.

There are two ways laypeople have traditionally helped start new churches. Sometimes, the church may begin a mission Sunday School or other extension ministry in another part of the city or neighboring community and ask its workers to assist on a short-term basis. The workers may retain their membership in the mother church and attend most of its services, but they agree to teach Sunday School or serve for a year or two in the new work until trained leaders can replace them. Sometimes, the extension workers may even be responsible for helping train their replacement before they return to the mother church.

A second approach, which often proves more effective, involves laypeople becoming an active part of the new church as part of its core membership. They become members of the new church on a permanent basis. Sometimes, people are already living in the target community and commute to the mother church each week. On other occasions, God gives people a burden for a community and they move to the new community as the new church is starting. When established churches use this approach to starting new churches, the new church gets a healthy start and often becomes self-supporting much faster. This approach is not without cost to the mother church as often its best leaders are among those who get involved with the new ministry, but most sending churches find God raises up new leaders to replace those who move on. Within a couple of years, one healthy church becomes two healthy churches making a great impact on two different communities. Some churches have been so impressed with this approach to church planting that they have a goal of beginning one new daughter church every five years.

Personal Lessons to Take Away

1. I can be used of God in ministry, even though I am a layperson.

2. I can advance to more responsibility and effectiveness in ministry by being faithful in my present ministry.

3. I can be used more effectively in some places in ministry than full-time ministers.

4. I can be used of God to help plant a new church, and then I can effectively minister in that new community.

5. I must be open to the call to full-time ministry, just as Philip was elevated to that task.

Church Lessons to Take Away

1. Laypersons who are ministering faithfully in the mother church successfully plant churches.

2. When laypeople get involved in ministry at a daughter church, they usually have made a commitment and taken a step of faith that qualifies them for greater spheres of ministry.

3. The key to successful church plants is the faithfulness of those laypersons involved in the daughter church.

4. Most laypersons involved in a daughter church plant will become involved in ministry and will grow in their walk with Christ.

5. Most laypersons involved in a new church plant will not remain nominal Christians, nor will they become in-

volved because of the convenience of location or availability of a church of similar denominational background.

6. The success of a new church plant is tied to the dedication, involvement, and spirituality of the laypeople involved in the daughter church.

Personal Projects

If your church were to start a new church, would you want a role as part of the ministry team? The Early Church realized every *member* of the church was also a *minister* in the church. Because everyone found their place on the ministry team, the Church was able to expand quickly into new communities. Without a significant involvement of laypeople in ministry, the growth of the Early Church would have been much slower.

Now it is our turn to put the Book of Acts back into action. As your church starts a new church, there will be plenty of ministry opportunities in both the mother church and daughter church. As you look for your place on the ministry team, use the following suggestions to help you apply what you have learned in this chapter.

1. Many Christians have reasons they believe exempt them from ministry. Often, these excuses reflect a lack of understanding of God's approach to ministry. Evaluate your own attitudes toward ministry. Then, ask God to help you find your place on the ministry team.

2. If you are not currently involved in a ministry, maybe it is time to get involved. Review the section titled *Finding a Ministry in Your Community* as a guideline to find a significant ministry in your church. As you join the ministry team, you will not only benefit as you grow in that ministry but also encourage others on the team who may currently be overworked.

3. Perhaps it is time for a new challenge in ministry. As your church begins a new church, it will need many of its finest leaders to step out by faith to be part of the ministry team in the new church. Does God want you to be part of

that team? Review the section *Finding a Community for Your Ministry,* and ask God to show you what role He has for you in your church's daughter church.

Church Project

One of the keys to a successful church plant is the quality of laypeople who help start the new daughter church. Therefore, the church planting team should spend time and energy recruiting others for the mother church to come help in the new project. Today's project involves identifying, contacting, recruiting, and enlisting other laypersons to join the church plant team.

Team Brainstorming—"Let's Get Help"

1. Bible reading.
   a. Read how Joshua involved workers. Josh. 1:10-18; 3:1-17; 6:1-27.
   b. Read how Nehemiah recruited help. Neh. 1:3-4; 2:1-20; 4:1-8, 13-23; 6:15-16.

2. Pray for help. Matt. 9:35-38.

3. Brainstorm: Make a "dream list" of all the ideal people you would need and like on the church plant team.

4. Share the dream with potential team members.
   a. Write a personal letter to potential team members to share your burden for the new church plant.
   b. Include a "vision statement" of the new church.
   c. Include any literature used to publicize the new church.
   d. Follow up the letter with a personal contact.

5. Share a testimony in the mother church by a layperson going to help start the new church plant. Pray that God will use the testimony to recruit helpers.

6. Place the names of individuals interested in planting the new church on the mail or E-mail list so they will receive all communications about the new church.

7. Continue to pray for new team members.

Team Brainstorming—Let's Use Everyone

Everyone on the ministry team has a spiritual gift (1 Cor. 12:11), so everyone should have a ministry. From the beginning, include all on the ministry team in visioning, planning, praying, and working. But don't force anyone into a task for which they are unqualified or nongifted. Use the following steps with the ministry team.

1. Include all members of the ministry team in visioning, that is, planning and writing the vision.
   a. Involve some on the committee that establishes the vision statement and/or ministry statement.
   b. Get everyone's input on the vision statement before adopting it.
2. Give a spiritual gift inventory to every member of the ministry team. (Visit www.elmertowns.com to find a spiritual gift inventory that your ministry team can use. It's free.)
   a. Have each person identify their three strongest spiritual gifts and their three weakest gifts. This will direct team members in areas where they should be ministering and areas where they should allow others to minister.
   b. Have a teaching session for the ministry team to explain the ministry gifts and how they can be used in planting a new church.
3. Revisit the committees you've established for the ministry team.
   a. Indicate what spiritual gifts fit best into each committee.
   b. Begin placing people in committees according to the spiritual gift of each.

5
Reaching Out to a Different Kind of People

The Church in Caesarea and Antioch

After Saul was converted, the intensity of the persecution against the Church subsided. The apostles were allowed to travel widely for ministry. Much had happened quickly in the first few years of the Church's existence in Jerusalem. Now, outside Jerusalem and Judea, a subtle shift in attitudes began to take place in some churches and among some church leaders. The Church in Jerusalem was a Jewish church. Even though Jesus had made it clear they would be witnesses to the whole world, their primary focus had been Jews (Acts 11:19). But things were beginning to change.

Philip's ministry in Samaria had been the first shock wave to hit the status quo. When word of the conversion of Samaritans first reached Jerusalem, the Church was not sure what to think. They decided to send two of their own, Peter and John, to investigate. The two were present when the Holy Spirit fell on the Samaritan church, and they could not help but see parallels between their earlier "Pentecost" experience and what happened in Samaria. When Jesus was in Sychar, He spoke with the woman at the well. It was there Jesus was first described as "the Savior of the world" (John 4:39-42). Although the Jews typically had no dealings with the Samaritans, the apostles were prepared to make an exception in this case based on the evident work of God in Samaritan lives. After all, Samaritans were "half-Jews."

Perhaps reaching Gentiles for Christ was impacting Peter more than he thought. With the decline in persecution, Peter traveled to several cities. When he arrived in Joppa, he stayed with a fellow believer named Simon. It had probably been the custom of Peter to stay in the homes of believers as he traveled, but Simon was a tanner. The very nature of working with dead animals and tanning hides made him unclean under Jewish law. Just a few years earlier, a more pious Peter might not have agreed to stay in his home. But a subtle change was beginning to take place in Peter.

Though the change in attitude toward people of different races had begun, it was still a long way from having an effect in the life of the whole Church. While Peter was praying on the roof of Simon's house one day, "he fell into a trance and saw heaven opened" (Acts 10:10-11). In this unusual vision, Peter saw a sheet lowered from heaven with all kinds of animals and insects on it, each of which he recognized as unclean based on the kosher food laws of the Old Testament. Then Peter heard the voice of God saying, "Rise, Peter; kill and eat" (v. 13).

"Surely something was wrong here," Peter thought. Perhaps he had not heard the voice correctly. It sounded as if God was telling him to eat the kind of food forbidden by Old Testament law. Peter might be staying in the home of a tanner, but he was not prepared to abandon his cultural values completely. "Not so, Lord!" he responded emphatically. Then with a touch of Jewish pride he added, "I have never eaten anything common or unclean" (v. 14).

What Peter had spoken with pride, God apparently viewed as part of the problem. "What God has cleansed you must not call common," the voice from heaven responded (v. 15).

This vision was repeated three times, leaving Peter thoroughly confused. As he thought about the vision, he heard a commotion downstairs as other guests were apparently arriving. Then Peter heard from God again. "The Spirit said to him, 'Behold, three men are seeking you. Arise therefore, go down and go with them, doubting nothing; for I have sent them'" (vv. 19-20).

Another Exception to the Rule

When Peter met the men, he learned they had been sent by a Roman centurion, that is, a Gentile. In light of the experience he had just had on the roof, he quickly agreed to accompany them to Caesarea. The new guests were invited to remain in Joppa for the evening so they could get a fresh start in the morning. The next morning, Peter and some of the Christians from the church in Joppa accompanied the men back to Caesarea.

When they arrived the next day, they found Cornelius an eager host, ready to greet them. When Peter entered the home of this Gentile, the centurion bowed down to worship him. Peter immediately objected, noting he, too, was only a man like his host.

The decision to enter the home of Cornelius went against everything Peter had been taught. "You know how unlawful it is for a Jewish man to keep company with or go to one of another nation," he reminded his host. "But God has shown me that I should not call any man common or unclean" (v. 28).

The centurion was convinced Peter would have something significant to say, so he had gathered a number of relatives and close personal friends to meet with Peter. As he introduced Peter to his assembled guests, Cornelius told Peter about a vision he had four days earlier that had prompted his inviting Peter. Then he announced, "We are all present before God, to hear all the things commanded you by God" (v. 33).

Like many of his fellow Jews, Peter still had a restricted view as to who could and could not win God's favor. Now Peter realized God was interested in the salvation of at least some Gentiles. Peter preached the life, death, and resurrection of Jesus. "To Him all the prophets witness that, through His name, whoever believes in Him will receive remission of sins" (v. 43).

No sooner had Peter spoken those words than "the Holy Spirit fell upon all those who heard the word" (v. 44). Christians who had accompanied Peter to Caesarea were astounded. Apparently, some in the group were among those converted to Christ in Jerusalem on the Day of Pentecost. They could not help but notice the similarities. Obviously, God had decided to visit them with a "Gentile Pentecost."

In light of what was taking place before their eyes, the Jewish Christians were prepared to accept the new Gentile Christians as brothers in Christ. Peter urged Cornelius, friends, and family to be baptized, and a predominantly Gentile church began in the city of Caesarea. Peter stayed a few days to help establish them in their newfound faith.

Word spread quickly about Peter's visit to Caesarea. By the time he returned to Jerusalem, he was confronted by those who had heard the rumor. "You went in to uncircumcised men and ate with them!" they accused (11:3).

Peter tried to explain his actions the best he could by recounting all the steps that had taken place beginning in Joppa. As the church leaders considered what Peter reported, they sat in silent amazement. Who among them would ever have thought God was interested in the conversion of Gentiles? What God did in Caesarea dawned on them. Their silence turned to approval (v. 18).

When the Exceptions Became the Rule

Had the apostles reasoned out the Great Commission, they no doubt would have concluded the conversion of Gentiles had to be in the plan of God. They would soon discover that Gentiles would become their biggest and most fruitful field of ministry. Maybe they considered Samaria and Caesarea the notable exceptions to the general rule of Jewish evangelism, but all that was about to change in Antioch.

If the conversion of Cornelius marked the beginning of Gentile evangelism, the church at Antioch became the first church to begin making the transition from being predominantly Jewish in character to becoming predominantly Gentile in its outlook. That change did not go unnoticed by the church in Jerusalem. When they heard about a Gentile church in Antioch, they decided to send someone to insure this church had not gone too far. Much of the Gentile outreach in Antioch had been started by men from Cyprus and Cyrene. Therefore, the church in Jerusalem sent Barnabas, who had Cypriot roots, to investigate.

Barnabas had already earned a reputation for being able to find the potential in people and build on it. He was the first to accept Saul of Tarsus after the zealous Pharisee had been converted. As Barnabas arrived in Antioch, he no doubt recognized some things were being done differently in the predominantly Gentile community. But he rejoiced in the evidences of God's grace at work in their midst "and encouraged them all that with purpose of heart they should continue with the Lord" (Acts 11:23).

As Barnabas preached in the church at Antioch, "a great many people were added to the Lord" (v. 24). Barnabas quickly realized that one of the problems confronting this church was directly related to their cultural background. In Jerusalem, most converts understood the Old Testament Scriptures well and had a basis upon which they could build their personal relationship with God. Here in Antioch, most new converts did not have this background. The greatest need of this church was a teacher who could instruct these Gentile converts in the Old Testament. As a Levite, Barnabas was no doubt capable of performing this ministry, but he remembered a young teacher who could do it much better.

Ten years earlier, Saul had headed back to Tarsus to escape the murderous plots of the Jews. Barnabas remembered Saul's zeal to teach the Old Testament Scriptures from a messianic perspective. So Barnabas made the trip to the Asian city of Tarsus to find Saul. "When he had found him, he brought him to Antioch" (v. 26a).

Together, Barnabas and Saul faithfully ministered to the disciples at Antioch during the next year. Many people were taught the Scriptures. Not only did the disciples of Antioch acquire an understanding of the Old Testament, but also they began to apply the eternal principles of the Scriptures to their own lifestyle. This resulted in their earning a reputation: "And the disciples were first called Christians in Antioch" (v. 26c).

An Ongoing Struggle for Some

First, there was Samaria. Then, Caesarea. Now, in Antioch God was working among non-Jews. It was quickly realized that God's plan for world evangelism meant moving beyond the comfort of the Jewish culture. It was not long before the church at Antioch sent some of its best people to establish new churches in other Gentile communities. Barnabas and Saul would be the first of many to take the message of the gospel beyond their city limits. When they returned from their first missionary journey, there was much rejoicing that the Gentiles were being saved.

But not everyone viewed the conversion of the Gentiles with the same enthusiasm. Among the Jews in Judea, there was still a strong feeling for the law. They were proud of their Jewish heritage, and it just didn't seem right that Gentiles could claim to be Christians like them, yet not value the Old Testament law. In their mind, something had to be done to correct this problem before things got completely out of control.

A group of Jewish Christians began traveling throughout Gentile churches teaching, "Unless you are circumcised according to the custom of Moses, you cannot be saved" (Acts 15:1). These men may have had the best of motives, but their message was terribly wrong. The addition of circumcision and other Jewish customs to the gospel challenged the essence of the gospel. Indeed, from the very beginning, the only conditions that had ever been tied to salvation were that people repent of their sin and trust Christ alone for salvation. Now, these Jewish Christian teachers were leading Gentile Christians into bondage that could only hinder their spiritual progress. As one might expect, this effort met with strong opposition from many Christian leaders. The controversy was so great, a special conference was held in Jerusalem to deal with the problem.

At the Jerusalem Conference, the issue was thoroughly discussed and a consensus was reached. Those gathered realized they could not in good conscience add anything to the gospel without polluting the integrity of the gospel itself. If a Gentile turned from his sin to trust Christ as Savior, that Gentile was just as saved as if he had been a Jew and done the same thing. Still, the Church realized some aspects of Gentile culture were especially offensive to the Jews they were still trying to reach. Just as they would not impose their Jewish heritage on Gentile converts, the Church asked Gentile converts to be aware of Jewish concerns and to abstain from food that had been offered to idols, from sexual immorality, and from eating meat that had been strangled or not properly bled. This concession on the part of Gentiles had nothing to do with their standing before God, but they would remove significant cultural barriers and make them more effective in reaching both Jews and Gentiles for Christ.

Why Can't People Be like Me?

Adjusting to a different culture can be difficult. An American missionary in South Korea had never seen chopsticks before his arrival in a small town to teach English to Buddhists. This was the missionary's means of building relationships to reach them for Christ. After a couple of frustrating meals, he decided to go buy a fork.

"I can't believe no one in town sold forks," he later complained. "I had to special-order a fork from Seoul, it took three months to arrive, and it ended up costing me $6.00 for one stainless steel fork. What's wrong with these people?" he asked.

Those who heard the missionary quickly realized there was nothing wrong with the South Koreans. He was just having difficulty adjusting to a new culture. His experience is not uncommon. Cultural shock is one big reason why some missionaries never return to the field for their second term of service. Their failure to recognize cross-cultural barriers prevents them from having a significant ministry.

The same attitude can also have a similar effect on our ministry in our community. As our world becomes increasingly cosmopolitan, people of other cultures are becoming our neighbors and coworkers. In cities like Miami, Philadelphia, and Toronto, the number of residents born outside the country far exceeds those born inside the country. In many other places, politicians recognize that the ability to communicate to those of a second, or in some cases a third, culture may be the difference between victory and defeat in the next election. Churches used to send missionaries into the whole world to preach the gospel. Now it seems as if the whole world has moved into our town.

Perhaps it is only natural that some respond by trying to impose their culture on the new immigrants. "If they are going to come here, they need to learn how to fit in with the rest of us," critics claim. "Why should we always be the ones to change?" they ask. "Don't they realize the reason they came here in the first place is because they liked what our country has to offer? If they don't like it now, then maybe they ought to go home!"

While there is much to be proud of in our culture, not the least of which is our Christian heritage, the frustrations behind these and similar statements is not unlike those of the missionary who had difficulty adjusting to chopsticks in a different culture. Like it or not, we live in a different world today. We can lament the fact and vent our frustrations, or we can look at our different world as an opportunity to do something great for God. Perhaps the real question we need to ask is, "How does God want us to use this opportunity to cross cultural barriers and reach a different kind of people with the gospel?"

Sometimes, going into all the world means staying home. The Great Commission is clear about making disciples of all nations (Matt. 28:19), going into all the world (Mark 16:15), preaching repentance and the remission of sins to all nations (Luke 24:47), and being Christ's witness "to the end of the earth" (Acts 1:8). But as the world continues moving to our hometown, it is becoming increasingly easier to have a global impact from home.

Who Lives in Your Town?

Effectively reaching a different kind of people now living in your town begins with an awareness of who actually lives there. Every decade, the national census surprises many as it reveals the shifting population patterns in our nation.

Most of us are creatures of habit. We live in similar neighborhoods even when we move to a new city. We tend to shop in the same store about the same time each week. As a result, we interact with the same people as the routine of our life rolls on. That is not a bad thing, but it may leave people thinking they know their community well when all they really know is that part of the community with which they interact on a regular basis. Who really lives on the other side of the tracks? And what about that new development on the edge of town? Who is buying all those new homes?

In most cities, city planners collect extensive demographic information to develop policy and attract new businesses to town. Many communities are prepared to share that information with anyone who asks for it. In some cases, there may be a slight fee for copying. However, copies of the latest demographics of your community may be available free in your public library.

As you examine that information, look for distinct "people groups" in your town. These are groups of people who have something significant in common. A church in Miami may realize there is a large Hispanic population in their community. But sometimes a people group may appear to blend in to its surroundings. That same church may overlook a large group of retired Canadians now living in their community. Or, an African-American church can overlook a large group of Haitians or Jamaicans just because they have the same color of skin.

As you think about the distinct people groups in your city, think beyond differences in language, race, and national origin. Consider the students at a local high school, college, or university. Each of these groups represents a subculture in your community. When you think about it, they have different kinds of needs. Listening to the radio may help you realize who is in your community. Music is a common reflection of the culture. People who listen to country tunes are often different from those who dial into the classical station. A "golden oldies" station in your community may suggest the presence of an aging baby boomer population.

No doubt, many churches have an effective ministry by limiting their focus to a homogeneous group. Their commitment to evangelizing their target group is to be commended. But how much greater would be the impact if they started new churches to reach across cultural barriers to evangelize a different kind of people.

Personal Lessons to Take Away

1. I am to overcome all negative attitudes of racism just as the Early Church did.

2. I must realize God loves people of different races and wants me to help reach those in different neighborhoods.

3. I may need to help teach biblical data and attitudes to those of different backgrounds from my own who are not grounded in biblical truth.

4. I must never let good works or religious customs become a substitute for the gospel.

5. I must be more open to people of different backgrounds than ever before and realize North America has more people of different racial backgrounds coming to our shores than ever before.

Church Lessons to Take Away

1. If we are to carry out the Great Commission to all our unreached neighbors, we must be willing to plant churches in neighborhoods different from our own.

2. We cannot plant a new church in a racially different neighborhood if we have negative attitudes toward people of a different race living in that neighborhood.

3. Planting a church in a neighborhood of people different from our present church may involve a strong teaching ministry of biblical truth (because people of different backgrounds may not have a basic biblical orientation to life).

4. We must begin looking, studying, and praying about planting a church among people of a different racial background from our church.

Personal Projects

The process of convincing a predominantly Jewish church to accept Gentiles as part of the family took time, but it happened. It happened because of the boldness of a group of Jewish Christians in Antioch who crossed cultural barriers to reach their Gentile neighbors. Although they did not realize it at the time, God was preparing them for a much larger ministry than they could imagine. While they wanted to reach their community for Christ, God wanted to use them to reach the world.

Now it is our turn to put the Book of Acts back into action. As you consider what you have learned in this chapter, how will it affect your life and church?

1. Some Christians today still have a hard time accepting people into their church from a different culture. What about you? If your church were to decide to be proactive in reaching out to a different kind of people, how comfortable would you be with that decision? Many are suspicious of people who are not the same color or speak the same language or eat the same food with us. As you review the process by which the Early Church began to embrace Gentiles, maybe you need to measure where your church is in accepting people from a different race or culture. If you struggle in this area, why not make this a matter of prayer in your personal quiet time this week?

2. Admittedly, it is uncomfortable to leave the security of our own culture to reach out to a different kind of people. Maybe this is a real area of struggle for you. Ponder your atti-

tudes. Even though they may not differ much from those in your church or community, if they are not addressed they could seriously limit the ministry potential God has for you or your church. Check off the reasons why you choose not to cross cultural barriers. Begin working on them one at a time.

3. How well do you really know your community? In this age of transition, the ethnic character of many communities is changing rapidly. For years, churches have sent missionaries to Asia, Africa, and Latin America. Today, many people from those regions are moving into our cities. Are they living in your community? If you're not sure, review the section titled *Who Lives in Your Town?* Ask God to show you in what part of town your church could start a new church. Talk to your pastor or Bible study group leader for practical suggestions to get started.

Church Project

1. As you continue to study about church planting, and as you focus more sharply on planting another church, you will want to consider the following:
   a. What different groups live near you?
   b. What is the size of the group?
   c. Is the group located in one general area, or are the people spread throughout your town or metropolitan area?

2. The ministry team will want some precise information on the different types of people groups in your area and in the neighborhoods your church could reach for Christ.
   a. Have a survey team or individual contact the agency in your area that has basic census data. (Chamber of Commerce, Better Business Bureau, City Planning Department, and so forth.)
   b. Visit the United States Census Bureau web site to find information on your area: www.census.gov
      • C2SS Profiles (Census 2000 Supplementary Survey web site)

- 2000 ACS Site Profiles (American Community Survey web site)

3. What (amount and types) of churches are already located among the various racial groups in your town or metropolitan area? (Contact the ministerial organization.)

4. What is being done by other denominations or interdenominational agencies to evangelize racial groups of people in your town or metropolitan area?

5. Appoint some class members to drive through an area where different racial groups are found. Have them do a "windshield survey" to determine what they see.
   - What churches are located there? (Size, number, types, and so forth.)
   - What and how many community service organizations are there?
   - What churches are found in those neighborhoods that are serving races other than the people found in that neighborhood?
   - Are there potential places to begin a church?
   - What are the conditions of the public schools? Municipal buildings?

6. Are there any members, visitors, or acquaintances to your church from the targeted neighborhood that could help in locating a Bible study, kids club, or similar?
   - Create a large map of the neighborhoods around your church, and place it on the wall of your classroom.
   - Note different people groups on your map as a prayer target.
   - Color different sections according to different people groups.
   - Use pins to indicate where families live from your church. Note those who could help reach a neighborhood with the gospel.

6
Plodding Through Problems with Purpose

The Churches of Galatia

Barnabas and Saul felt the call of God to take the gospel to other cities in which there was no Christian church. As they prayed about this matter, God confirmed their call to their church at Antioch. When there were a number of leaders in Antioch who were fasting together, "the Holy Spirit said, 'Now separate to Me Barnabas and Saul for the work to which I have called them'" (Acts 13:2). After a further fasting, the church agreed that these two men should be their missionary representatives. Thus Barnabas and Saul were sent on the first missionary journey. Barnabas's nephew, John Mark, who was in Antioch, joined the mission team, probably to look after the various details of travel and lodging.

Barnabas and Saul began their mission trip by taking a ship to Cyprus. Barnabas had sold his real estate holdings on the island of Cyprus several years earlier, but he still likely had contact with old friends and associates on the island. Also, several members of the church in Antioch had their roots on the Mediterranean island (Acts 11) and may have notified their friends and relatives to prepare for the coming of the apostles.

When Barnabas and Saul arrived at Salamis in Cyprus, they made their way to the synagogues to preach the gospel. Wherever there were 12 Jewish families in a Gentile city, the Jews were required to build a synagogue. These buildings served as Jewish community centers in Gentile cities as a gathering place of Jews. Jewish children were taught in synagogues. Throughout the apostles' ministry, they found the gospel was best introduced to a city through the synagogue. Using this approach, Barnabas and Saul worked their way across the island until they came to Paphos, the island's capital city.

Facing Satanic Problems

In Paphos, the team encountered a satanic opposition. A local Jew named Elymas, also called Bar-Jesus, had embraced the occult religion of the area, becoming a false prophet practicing sorcery. He served as a spiritual adviser to the Roman proconsul of the area, Sergius Paulus. When the proconsul learned of Barnabas's and Saul's presence, he asked them to come explain God's Word to him more clearly. They agreed but were opposed in their efforts by Elymas, who was "seeking to turn the proconsul away from the faith" (Acts 13:8). In the face of the opposition, Saul turned to the sorcerer to perform what was probably his first miracle: "O full of all deceit and all fraud, you son of the devil, you enemy of righteousness, will you not cease perverting the straight ways of the Lord? And now, indeed, the hand of the Lord is on you, and you shall be blind, not seeing the sun for a time" (vv. 10-11).

Immediately, the sorcerer lost his sight and had to be led around by others. When the proconsul saw this demonstration of the power of God, he believed in Jesus as his personal Savior. This miracle seemed to elevate Saul above Barnabas in the eyes of those who saw it. Whereas Barnabas's name had appeared first in the biblical text, from now on Paul's name would appear first. From this time, Saul's Hebrew name was abandoned, and he was identified by his Gentile name, Paul. Also, from this point on, Paul would have a wider ministry as the apostle to the Gentiles.

Shortly after the conversion of Sergius Paulus, the mission team decided to leave Cyprus to evangelize Asia Minor, today called Turkey. When they arrived in Perga, John Mark left the group to return home. While the reason for his departure is not stated in Scripture, many Bible teachers believe he may have become frustrated as Paul assumed a bigger leadership role over his uncle Barnabas. Also, the missionary team was plunging deeper into Gentile territory, all the time getting farther away from the Holy Land. John Mark's departure was not on good terms. When Paul and Barnabas discussed a second missions tour years later, Paul strongly opposed taking John Mark, even to the point of breaking with Barnabas, who wanted to give his nephew a second chance.

Paul and Barnabas traveled north to Antioch in Pisidia (a different city from Antioch of Syria, the city they left). When they attended the synagogue on the Sabbath, they were invited to address the gathering. Paul accepted the invitation and preached the gospel. He concluded his message by telling the people, "that through this Man is preached to you the forgiveness of sins; and by Him everyone who believes is justified from all things from which you could not be justified by the law of Moses" (vv. 38-39).

The response to Paul's message was extremely positive. Many Jews and proselytes believed Jesus was the Messiah. As word spread through town that week about what had taken place, interest continued to grow. When the apostles returned to the synagogue the next week, "almost the whole city came together to hear the word of God" (v. 44).

Facing Rejection

Unfortunately, the success of the apostles in attracting a large crowd also aroused a jealous streak in the Jewish leaders. During the meeting, they rose to oppose all the apostles said. When Paul realized what was going on, he suggested they would take the message directly to the Gentiles. This was well received by the Gentiles but only further angered the Jewish leaders. They began pulling political strings to have the two expelled from their region. Paul and Barnabas left but not without leaving behind a church, that is, a joyous group of disciples.

From Antioch, the pair continued traveling inland to Iconium. Again they preached in the synagogue and saw many Jews and Gentiles express faith in Christ. And once again, the

Jews who rejected their message turned against the mission team. This time they plotted with hostile Gentiles to stone the apostles. When the apostles heard of the plot, they escaped unharmed and began preaching in Lystra, Derbe, and other parts of the region.

Facing Persecution and Death

At Lystra, Paul healed a man who had been crippled from birth. When the people saw the miracle, they assumed the apostles were the incarnation of two gods, Zeus and Hermes. As the priests of Zeus came out to sacrifice to Paul and Barnabas, the apostles tore their clothes to reject the sacrifice and spoke to the crowd to restrain them. They claimed they, too, were mortal men and urged the crowd to turn from their idols to serve the living God. While there is no report of people converted at the time, the apostles were successful in ending the sacrifice.

It was not long, however, when the Jews who had opposed Paul and Barnabas in Antioch and Iconium found the apostles in Lystra. They incited the people. Paul was stoned, and his body was dragged out of the city. They left Paul for dead, but he got up a short time later, bruised but very much alive. Some Bible teachers believe the apostle actually died on the occasion and was restored to life to continue his ministry.

Those who believe Paul actually died in Lystra point to the apostle's description of his after-death experience in his Second Epistle to the Corinthians. During this time, Paul "was caught up into Paradise and heard inexpressible words, which it is not lawful for a man to utter" (12:4). This experience was so personally significant that Paul felt uncomfortable sharing it with others until 14 years after the fact. Paul, who had at least five visions in which he saw Jesus after the Resurrection, apparently looked upon this experience as the most significant one. He understood the experience could lead him into pride and distract him from the primary focus of his ministry.

Because of this, Paul believed he had been given what he called "a thorn in the flesh . . . a messenger of Satan to buffet me" (v. 7). Nowhere does the Scripture specifically identify the nature of this thorn, but it was apparently irritating enough that Paul "pleaded with the Lord three times that it might depart from [him]" (v. 8). On each occasion, the Lord's response to that prayer was, "My grace is sufficient for you, for My strength is made perfect in weakness" (v. 9). As a result, Paul not only learned to accept this problem but also came to appreciate it as the means of securing grace for his ministry.

The next day after Paul was stoned, Paul and Barnabas headed for Derbe, where they again preached the gospel and saw many converted to the faith. They retraced their steps to visit the new churches on their way home to Antioch in Syria, "strengthening the souls of the disciples, exhorting them to continue in the faith," and reminding them that tribulations would precede their entering into the kingdom of God (Acts 14:22).

Their first missions tour was successful in opening "the door of faith to the Gentiles" (v. 27), but it had not been without problems. By the end of the journey, Paul knew that problems facing him and new churches were not over. Paul realized every problem was worth the privilege that was his to preach the gospel to people who had never heard it before.

Why Troubles Come!

Nobody likes problems, but problems are a reality of life. Friction always accompanies motion. Still, in the midst of our problems, the most common question is *why?* "Why me?" "Why now?" "Why this?" While some people look for a simple answer to explain every problem, the Bible suggests many reasons why people experience problems in life. We may experience different problems for different reasons.

Even when we know why God has allowed a problem to enter into our lives, we still need to be alert to how problems may affect us. In the midst of his problems, Job experienced the mental anguish of confusion (10:15). At times he found himself drained emotionally and experiencing a significant loss of energy (30:16). Difficult situations in life may result in intense crying and grief (Ps. 88:9) or even discouragement and extended periods of depression (Prov. 15:13). Many people find it difficult to continue trusting God in the face of a problem that just seems to drag on (Ps. 38:17).

But even when it seems as if God is silent, He does not abandon us in our problems. No matter what the situation, we can be assured the pressures we face are limited to what God knows we can handle (1 Cor. 10:13). He ensures there is a way by which we are able to bear up under the most intense problems. Sometimes, God intervenes to deliver us from our troubles (Ps. 34:19). More often, God comforts us in the midst of our problems, preparing us for something greater (2 Cor. 1:4).

24 Responses to Problems

In the event God chooses not to rescue us, we need to learn how to live through problems. A wise pastor once said, "One of three things is true. Either you are now in the midst of a problem, or you have just come out of a problem, or any day now you are in for the surprise of your life!" The key to a successful Christian life and ministry is found not in avoiding problems but in learning how to deal with them. The Scriptures suggest two dozen ways Christians can respond to problems.

1. Begin by asking God to forgive any known or unknown sin in your life that has not yet been dealt with (Ps. 25:18).

2. Steadfastly resist the devil (1 Pet. 5:9).

3. Listen to the warnings of God to minimize your pain (Acts 20:23).

4. Understand the role of suffering as part of the normal Christian experience in shaping us to become all God intends us to be (Ps. 34:19).

5. Learn to value suffering (1 Pet. 3:13-17).

6. Make a conscious choice to live through pain and suffering for God's glory (Heb. 11:25).

7. Always be aware of God's full appreciation of your situation (Ps. 106:44).

8. Let your ultimate hope balance your awareness of your problem (Rom. 8:18).

9. You may find it helpful to remember how God has delivered you from other significant problems in the past (Pss. 77:11-12; 78:42).

10. Remain conscious of God's unconditional love for you even in the midst of your pain (Rom. 8:35).

11. Resist the natural tendency to be overcome with fear (Rev. 2:10).

12. Instead, let your pain and suffering humble you before God (2 Chron. 33:12).

13. If necessary, express your concerns and desires frankly to God (Deut. 26:7).

14. Remain confident of God's ability to deal with your difficulty in the way most likely to bring glory to himself (2 Tim. 1:12).

15. Consciously commit yourself to God's care in the midst of your circumstance (1 Pet. 4:19).

16. Be patient in the midst of your problems; it's one of the toughest things to do (Rom. 12:12).

17. Be encouraged with the examples of others who have experienced problems in their lives (James 5:10).

18. Study how others lived through problems; it will help you stay faithful to God in the midst of your darkest hours (Rev. 2:10).

19. Find comfort in the Scriptures (Ps. 119:50, 92).

20. Remain teachable even in the worst of times (Ps. 119:71).

21. Learn to look beyond your own problems to find ways to minister to the needs of others (Eph. 3:13).

22. Worship God in your problems (Exod. 4:31).

23. Use music to help you drive your sorrows away (Isa. 51:11).

24. Even when it is hard, rejoice and find joy in what God is accomplishing in your life through a present difficulty (James 1:2).

Growing a Ministry out of Problems

When Paul and Barnabas returned to Antioch to report on the success of their first missions tour, the sending church rejoiced over what God had done. There may have been some, however, who wondered how much better things might have been if there had not been so many problems. That was probably not Paul's view. Throughout his Epistles, Paul taught Christians to learn to value problems as the fertile soil out of which a rich ministry grows.

As Paul began writing the Second Epistle to the Corinthians, he described God as "the Father of mercies and God of all comfort" (1:3). He explained God "comforts us in all our tribulation, that we may be able to comfort those who are in any trouble, with the comfort with which we ourselves are comforted by God" (v. 4). To have an effective ministry with people who hurt, sometimes you need to hurt first. The answers people need in their trouble don't come from books about problems, but our problems will help us learn so we can share our experience with those in the midst of problems. Those working out in the gym remember the motto, "No pain; no gain." The same might be said of those in ministry.

One of those converted to Christ during Paul's difficult ministry in Lystra (where he was stoned) was Timothy, a young man who later joined his mission team. When Paul later wrote Timothy to encourage him in ministry, he reminded Timothy of what the young man had seen in Paul's ministry and urged him to trust God for the same victory. "But you have carefully followed my doctrine, manner of life, purpose, faith, longsuffering, love, perseverance, persecutions, afflictions, which happened to me at Antioch, at Iconium, at Lystra—what persecutions I endured. And out of them all the Lord delivered me" (2 Tim. 3:10-11).

Personal Lessons to Take Away

1. I can be called of God to help plant new churches.

2. I will face satanic opposition when I help plant a new church, so I must rely on God's power to keep me and use me.

3. I must realize that planting a new church will not be easy, so I must be willing to face some satanic opposition.

4. I will face personal persecution and problems as I help plant a new church, so I must be willing to endure them and find ways to solve them.

5. I must realize all opposition is only allowed by God; He has a purpose for all the difficulties I endure.

6. Whatever problems or difficulties I will face, God has a "way of escape" to help me endure them.

Church Lessons to Take Away

1. A church can plant another church by sending out people from its congregation to do it.

2. New churches are best planted when some of the best workers from the mother church are sent to begin a new church, not sending those who are troublemakers or non-workers.

3. There will be satanic opposition against a new church plant.

4. People in the neighborhood where you plant a new church will oppose evangelistic efforts by a new church.

5. There will be persecution and hardships suffered by those who go to plant a new church.

6. In spite of opposition, the joy and results of church planting are worth the difficulties.

7. God gives reasons and a "way of escape" to those who suffer difficulty when they plant a new church.

Personal Projects

When a Bible school student learned a minister had started several churches, he thought that was "a cool ministry." "Not really," the church planter responded. "Sometimes church planting was just a lot of hard work and a lot of disappointments." While we can get excited about planting a new church, it is also important to remember that such a ministry undertaking is not without problems. God wants us to count the costs before we begin. We need to be aware problems are coming without letting those problems discourage us. Rather, problems provide great opportunities to watch God act on our behalf.

Now it's our turn to put the Book of Acts back into action. As you look for ways to apply what you have been learning in this chapter, use the following suggestions to address your problems and keep plodding forward to accomplish God's purpose in and through your life.

1. How do you respond when you find yourself face-to-face with a problem? Do you find yourself asking the "Why?" questions for which it seems there are no answers. Consider some of the reasons why God may allow problems in your life. Do any of these reasons speak to specific situations in your life? Take time to thank God for bringing problems into your life.

2. Maybe right now, you find yourself in the midst of a major crisis. Remember, if God allowed it to happen, He believes you can handle it. You may wish God did not have such a high opinion of your ability. Read the section titled *24 Responses to Problems* to gain insight into specific ways God may want you to cope with your present situation. Although you may feel like hiding, you probably need to discuss your situation with a good Christian friend who will pray for you and encourage you as you work through this process.

3. As you begin thinking about problems that you may experience as your church starts a new church, you may be tempted to jump ship before it gets out of the harbor. Paul

probably felt like that at times, but he grew to realize the most effective ministry grows out of problems. Review the section titled *Growing a Ministry out of Problems,* and try to apply those principles to your situation.

Church Project

When you make preparations to plant a new church, the team should be aware of the different types of opposition they will face and the different degrees of suffering they will have to endure. Along with this lesson, the team should have a frank discussion of their opposition and how they will respond.

Team Meetings—"Counting the Cost"

1. Bible reading.
   a. Read what Jesus said about endurance:
      His suffering, Luke 9:21-22
      His challenge to discipleship, Luke 9:23-26
      His experience and compassion, Luke 9:51-56
      His test, Luke 9:57-62
   b. Read what Paul endured, 2 Cor. 4:8-11
   c. Read what Peter said about suffering, 1 Pet. 4:1-19
2. Discuss what opposition you will face and how you will react.
   a. From antagonistic individuals
   b. From the neighborhood
   c. From authorities
   d. From other churches
   e. From satanic sources
3. Discuss your strategy to answer opposition before it comes.
   a. How will the group "be wise as serpents and harmless as doves" (Matt. 10:16)?
   b. How will you pray for success?
   c. How will you be a good testimony for Christ?
4. Discuss how you will use the mother church to help eliminate opposition.

7

Reaching Your Personal Sphere of Influence

The Church at Philippi

The second missionary journey began when Paul chose Silas to go with him. Because Silas had proven himself a capable leader in both Jerusalem and Antioch, the new team was "commended by the brethren [at Antioch] to the grace of God" as they began their ministry trip (Acts 15:40).

When Paul returned to Galatia (modern-day Turkey), he found a strong, well-established church in Derbe and Lystra. A young man named Timothy had risen to a place of prominence. Both his mother and grandmother were Christians who had nurtured and encouraged Timothy. Because he had a good reputation among the Christians, Paul invited him to join his ministry team (probably doing the task John Mark did on the first trip).

Paul and the team traveled from church to church and "delivered to them the decrees to keep, which were determined by the apostles and elders at Jerusalem" (16:4). This resulted in both a deepening of the Christian experience of the believers and a numerical increase in the growth of the church as others were reached for Christ.

The team set off across Asia Minor (Turkey) but were frustrated because the Holy Spirit kept closing doors. They continued traveling west, looking for alternative fields of ministry. "After they had come to Mysia, they tried to go into Bithynia, but the Spirit did not permit them" (v. 7). They traveled across Asia Minor, not being able to find any open doors. They ended up at the port city of Troas, not really sure what to do next. In Troas, two things gave them new direction.

First, Luke the physician joined the missionary team. Although Luke, the author of the third Gospel, never identifies himself by name, he does change his writing style. In describing the team coming to Troas, he uses the third person plural "they" (v. 8). But when describing their departure, he uses the first person plural "we" (v. 10).

The second thing that happened in Troas was a vision Paul experienced that has become known as "the Macedonian Call." Paul had probably heard stories of people in Europe from Luke or others in the busy port city of Troas. But in a vision Paul saw a man from Macedonia standing and pleading, "Come over to Macedonia and help us" (v. 9). This vision was unique in Paul's experience, but everyone on the team agreed on its meaning. Immediately, the team secured passage from Troas to Macedonia. They boarded a ship that took them on a straight course from Troas to the island of Samothrace. The next day, they sailed on to Neapolis. From there, the team traveled inland to the colony of Philippi.

Paul's Ministry in Philippi

The city of Philippi was located about nine miles inland from the seaport of Neapolis. The city had been captured and fortified in 358 B.C. by Philip II, the father of Alexander the Great, and named in his honor. Philip sought control of the city because of the fertile soil nearby, the valuable gold mines in the region, and its strategic position in the event of an invasion from Asia.

There was not a large Jewish community in the city, so the few Jews and some ladies met at the river for prayer. Apparently there was no synagogue. Since Roman colonies tended to insist upon practices that the Jews found offensive like emperor worship, Jews tended not to settle in places like Philippi. The group that met by the river appears to have been almost exclusively women. As they met by the river, Paul and his ministry team met to pray and worship with them.

Paul had an immediate opportunity to preach the gospel without interference. One of those present in the group was a recent immigrant from Thyatira, a businesswoman named Lydia. She was involved in the fashion industry and is described as "a seller of purple," which probably means she dealt largely with the upper-class citizens of the city in her business (Acts 16:14). She and her household were the first to respond positively to the gospel. Upon her conversion, she immediately invited the ministry team to accept her hospitality as long as they stayed in the city.

The team continued their ministry for some time, working primarily with the riverside prayer group. But these were not the only religious people in that city. There was also "a certain slave girl possessed with a spirit of divination . . . who brought her masters much profit by fortune-telling" (v. 16). As she watched the team go to the river, she announced to all who would listen, "These men are the servants of the Most High God, who proclaim to us the way of salvation" (v. 17).

Initially, Paul and his team simply ignored her and carried on their ministry in spite of her interference. After several days Paul turned and said, "I command you in the name of Jesus Christ to come out of her" (v. 18). Immediately, the girl was released from the bondage of the spirit. While this meant she would no longer be an annoyance to the mission team, it also meant she no longer had the ability to predict the future and could therefore no longer make money for her owners.

Angry over their financial loss, the owners of the slave girl had Paul and Silas arrested, claiming, "These men, being Jews, exceedingly trouble our city; and they teach customs which are not lawful for us, being Romans, to receive or observe" (vv. 20-21). The Romans were apparently successful in having Paul and Silas imprisoned because of the anti-Semitic attitude that was at this time sweeping through the Roman Empire. But neither Timothy nor Luke, who had Gentile fathers, were arrested, even though they were members of the ministry team.

City officials immediately ordered Paul and Silas to be "beaten with rods" (v. 22) without making any further inquiries as to their guilt or innocence. Then they were turned over to the jailer, who was ordered to keep them secure. Assuming the men were dangerous prisoners, he locked "their feet in the stocks" located in the inner prison (v. 24). Although the day had begun like any other, the setting sun found Paul and Silas in a cold, damp Roman prison. Rather than feel sorry for themselves, Paul and Silas responded by "praying and singing hymns to God" (v. 25).

The prayers and singing were loud enough that others in the prison could hear what they were doing. By midnight, the whole prison was apparently listening to the two Jewish teachers. Suddenly, the singing was drowned out by an earthquake. The prison walls swung from side to side. By the time the earthquake ended, every lock in the jail was opened. Every prisoner was free from his chains, and all the doors were open.

The jailer himself had been sleeping when the earthquake began but quickly awakened. When he went into the jail to inspect the damage, he recognized his worst nightmare had come to pass. Seeing the open doors of the jail, he assumed the prisoners had all escaped. He knew the penalty for letting prisoners escape and realized his superior would not accept the earthquake as an excuse. The easiest way out of this situation was to take his own life immediately. The escape would cost him his life eventually.

As he drew his sword to kill himself, the jailer heard a voice. "Do yourself no harm, for we are all here," the voice cried out (v. 28). Calling for a light, the jailer went to see for himself. It was true. None of the prisoners had escaped, including the two who had been delivered to him that afternoon. Obviously shaken from the events, he brought Paul and Silas out of the jail into his own home. There he asked, "Sirs, what must I do to be saved?" (v. 30). The men answered the jailer, "Believe on the Lord Jesus Christ, and you will be saved, you and your household" (v. 31).

The jailer, his family, and servants continued to listen to Paul and Silas explain the gospel as they cleaned the men's wounded backs. By the time the prisoners' wounds had been dressed, the jailer and his household had come to believe what they had been taught. That night they were baptized. When they returned to the jailer's home, the jailer sat the two men at his table to feed them, rejoicing in his newfound faith in Christ.

The next morning, the city officials sent word to the jail that Paul and Silas could be released. When the apostles learned of the decision, they refused to accept the conditions of the release. "They have beaten us openly, uncondemned Romans, and have thrown us into prison. And now do they put us out secretly? No indeed! Let them come themselves and get us out," Paul explained (v. 37).

When the officers carried this message back to the magistrates, they were afraid and immediately came to the jail. Under Roman law, anyone possessing Roman citizenship was given certain rights that could not be refused. One of these rights involved freedom from punishment without due process of law. The magistrates knew they could be in serious trouble if Paul and Silas pressed for an investigation into the abuse of their rights as citizens. They arrived to plead with them to leave the city. Paul and Silas agreed to do so, but not before they returned to Lydia's home to encourage the church.

The Conversion of Households

In describing the effectiveness of Paul's ministry in Philippi, Luke uses the Greek word *oikos* twice (Acts 16:15, 31). This word literally means "house" but is also used to describe the members of the family, extended family, or household. This included those related to one another by blood or marriage. A household could also include servants of the family, close friends who often visited, and even business associates who came to the home to buy or sell merchandise. Basically an *oikos* household described more than the family; it included the social network of the person.

Reaching people through a network of existing relationships was one reason why the Early Church was so effective in evangelism. In addition to the conversion of the household of Lydia and the Philippian jailer, the New Testament describes the conversion of Cornelius's household (Acts 10:7, 24) as well as that of Crispus, the ruler of the synagogue in Corinth (18:8). When later writing to the Corinthians, Paul mentions having "baptized the household of Stephanas" about the same time as the conversion of Crispus (1 Cor. 1:16).

Paul was not the only one who took advantage of evangelizing through existing social networks. Jesus used relationships to gather the 12 disciples. The first 2 to follow Him were Andrew and John, who were previously disciples of His cousin John the Baptist (John 1:35-37). Each of these men was responsible for bringing his brother, Simon Peter and James respectively, into the fold (v. 41). The next day, Jesus invited Philip to become His disciple, who was from Andrew and Peter's hometown (v. 43). Philip then introduced his friend Nathanael to Jesus (v. 46).

Identifying Your Personal Sphere of Influence

A research poll of non-Christians with no church affiliation discovered 80 percent claimed they would attend church services if invited by a friend. Reaching people in their personal sphere of influence is the most effective way to reach people for Christ. But then, it has always been that way. When Lydia came to faith in Christ, others in her household were also saved. When the Philippian jailer trusted Christ, others in his household followed his example. Just as Jesus used existing social networks to gather His disciples, so He can use your existing social networks to make you an effective witness for Him.

The first step to use in incorporating *oikos evangelism* is to identify your personal sphere of influence. These are the people you touch or influence. You can reach them for Christ. Those in our personal sphere of influence include friends, relatives, associates, and neighbors, called FRANs.[1]

---

1. Elmer Towns, *FRANtastic Days* (Lynchburg, Va: Church Growth Institute, 1983), 63. A resource album containing four audiotapes, instructions, lesson plans, a planning calendar, trans-

Start with your own family. As you think about your extended family, list those who are related to you by blood and marriage who do not have a personal relationship with our Lord Jesus Christ. This group includes your parents, siblings, spouse, and children. But it reaches beyond your immediate family to include aunts, uncles, cousins, nieces, nephews, grandparents, grandchildren, great-grandchildren, and in-laws. In many cultures, the family may also include relatives who are several generations removed, that is, second or third cousins. If you are the only Christian in your family, you may have many family members to add to your list. If you come from a Christian home, your list of unsaved family members may be very small.

Next, consider your associates. Your associates include those with whom you rub shoulders on a fairly regular basis. Your list might include people you associate with in a workplace or school setting, people you regularly meet through routine activities such as commuting, shopping, working out, and so forth, and people you know through mutual involvement in various community activities. Don't forget your children's teachers and coaches of the sports teams they join. You may also want to include people you know through your involvement in a local political party or similar organization.

Your list may be getting long, but don't quit until you include neighbors. Think beyond the families whose homes are on either side of yours. In some communities, you may know people living a block away better than you know a neighbor. As one man thought about his personal sphere of influence, it took him a long time to list his neighbors. He was a build-

---

parency masters, student work sheets, and advertisement masters. This is a campaign that emphasizes reaching FRANs (i.e., friends, relatives, associates, and neighbors). The campaign is four weeks long, one Sunday to invite each person represented by the word FRAN. Follow-up of visitors in this campaign uses The Law of Three Hearings and The Law of Seven Touches. It emphasizes networking evangelism.

ing superintendent in an apartment building with over a hundred units. Because the building was older, he was often in people's apartments fixing leaking pipes. As you consider those you know living in your immediate community, list those who are not Christian.

Before you put your pen down, don't forget to list your friends. You may have some friends who really do not fit into one of the three groups already surveyed. List each one who is not a Christian.

As you work through this process, many on your list are more likely to consider the gospel if they hear it from you. What an opportunity! As you look over this list, remember one key to success in witnessing is to talk to God about people before talking to people about God. Begin praying daily for those listed in your sphere of influence. As you pray, invite the Holy Spirit to work conviction in their hearts, causing them to see their need for Christ (John 16:7-11). Also, ask God to give you an opportunity to share your faith with them and grant you the courage to do it when the opportunity arises (Col. 4:3-4).

Enlist others to join you in praying for those in your sphere of influence. Jesus promised, "If two of you agree on earth concerning anything that they ask, it will be done for them by My Father in heaven" (Matt. 18:19). Therefore, find others who will pray with you for the salvation of those in your sphere of influence. You may want to share prayer lists so that each is praying for the other.

Developing an Effective Evangelistic Prayer Strategy

Charles Haddon Spurgeon once described prayer as "the slender nerve that moves the arm of the Omnipotent." R. A. Torrey argued, "Prayer can do anything God can do, and as God can do anything, prayer is omnipotent." But many Christians sense their personal prayer life is anemic rather than all-powerful.

The Christian wanting answers from God should be careful to meet the various conditions for effective prayer. First,

God responds to prayers offered by those who are yielded to His will (1 John 5:14). Second, God responds to prayers that are prayed with faith (Mark 11:24). Third, God responds to prayers that are offered by those persistent in prayer (Col. 4:2). Also, God responds to prayers offered in sincerity (Ps. 145:18). A fifth condition of effective prayer is reverence for God (v. 19).

At times, the intensity with which one prays can also be a factor influencing God's response to prayer (Acts 12:5; Rom. 15:30; Col. 4:12). Agreement or unity among Christians is yet another factor impacting the effectiveness of prayer (Matt. 18:19). Eighth, God responds to the prayers of those who are humble before Him (Ps. 10:17). Abiding in Christ and the Word of God is a ninth condition of effective prayer (John 15:7). Finally, God responds to prayer made "in Jesus' name," which means prayer is answered for Jesus' sake rather than any merit in the one praying (14:13-14; 15:16).

Seven Ways to Undermine an Effective Prayer Life

Just as certain conditions can enhance the effectiveness of prayer, so other conditions may hinder the effectiveness of prayer. As you pray for the unsaved in your personal sphere of influence, you want to be sure you are not doing things that may undermine your prayer ministry.

Any unconfessed sin will hinder the effectiveness of prayer. The psalmist acknowledged, "If I regard iniquity in my heart, the Lord will not hear" (Ps. 66:18). Likewise, the prophet Isaiah wrote, "Behold, the LORD's hand is not short-ened, that it cannot save; nor His ear heavy, that it cannot hear. But your iniquities have separated you from your God; and your sins have hidden His face from you, so that He will not hear" (59:1-2).

Rejecting the known will of God will also hinder the effec-tiveness of prayer. The Bible says, "One who turns away his ear from hearing the law, even his prayer is an abomination" (Prov. 28:9). When you consider the other things described as "an abomination" in Scripture, that's pretty strong language.

Wrong motives impede true prayer. That is what James was talking about when he wrote, "You ask and do not receive, because you ask amiss, that you may spend it on your pleasures" (4:3).

Harboring idols in your heart will also hinder the effectiveness of your prayer. God's message to Israel through the prophet Ezekiel was, "Son of man, these men have set up their idols in their hearts, and put before them that which causes them to stumble into iniquity. Should I let Myself be inquired of at all by them?" (14:3). Although few Christians today may own idol shelves like those in Israel at the time, many may still be guilty of idolatry in the heart. An idol in your heart is anything about which you are more passionate than you are toward God. The Great Commandment calls us to love God supremely. When something gets in the way between you and God, it becomes an idol in your heart.

Prayer is also hindered by an unforgiving spirit. When Jesus taught His disciples about the prayer of faith, He said, "And whenever you stand praying, if you have anything against anyone, forgive him, that your Father in heaven may also forgive you your trespasses. But if you do not forgive, neither will your Father in heaven forgive your trespasses" (Mark 11:25-26).

Ignoring the needs of the poor will hinder the effectiveness of prayer. According to Solomon, "Whoever shuts his ears to the cry of the poor will also cry himself and not be heard" (Prov. 21:13).

Your prayer life may also hindered by domestic conflict. In discussing relationships between husbands and wives, Peter wrote, "Likewise you husbands, dwell with them with understanding, giving honor to the wife, as to the weaker vessel, and as being heirs together of the grace of life, that your prayers may not be hindered" (1 Pet. 3:7).

God has placed you in the midst of an unsaved world to make an eternal difference in the lives of others. The key to successfully rising to that challenge is to always talk to God about people, then talk to people about God.

Personal Lessons to Take Away

1. I can reach and win my friends, relatives, associates, and neighbors for Christ more effectively than strangers or other Christians not known to them.

2. I will be more effective when I witness to those within my existing network of relationships.

3. I should be interceding for the salvation of those in my existing web of relationships, because they will be most receptive to my testimony.

4. Not everyone I know will receive Christ, but they will probably be more receptive to my witness than to others.

5. While it is difficult to witness, I have a responsibility to share my faith with those that I know best.

6. If I cannot pray effectively about general items, I will have difficulty praying for my FRANs.

Church Lessons to Take Away

1. A church grows when they reach and keep lost people through existing relationships of its members.

2. Churches should target for evangelism those prospects who are within the existing networks of its present members.

3. Churches should use the majority of its energy and resources trying to evangelize those lost people within the social web of its members.

4. Churches should plan to pray in a constant and systematic way for the unsaved FRANs of its members.

Personal Projects

It is time once again to put the Book of Acts into action. The church at Philippi began with the riverside prayer group meeting. It grew as households came to faith in Christ, with people reaching others through their personal sphere of influence. As you consider this pattern of ministry, choose one of the following projects to help you become a practitioner of what you have learned.

1. Do you have a list of unsaved people for whom you are praying daily? Review the section titled *Identifying Your Personal Sphere of Influence*. As you read, compile your own prayer list of FRANs; then be alert to opportunities to witness to those on your prayer list.

2. Have you ever decided to lose weight without telling anyone and found yourself 10 pounds heavier two months later? Most of us need someone to hold us accountable if we are going to stick to the task at hand. Who is holding you accountable to be faithful in praying for unsaved friends, relatives, associates, and neighbors? If you do not have a couple of prayer partners, set a goal to find one this week. Then look for someone else to join the two of you in a prayer triplet.

3. How effective is your prayer life? Review the section titled *Seven Ways to Undermine an Effective Prayer Life*. Let God speak to you about your prayer life. Then respond to Him in prayer, confessing where you fall short and asking Him for grace to grow in this important spiritual discipline.

Church Projects

1. Plan a "Friend Day" activity for the new embryonic church you are planning. This could be a luncheon, picnic, sports activity, musical concert, or similar. Have all of the members of the ministry team make a list of 10 people they could invite to this event. The purpose of the event is not evangelistic, Bible teaching, or recruitment for church membership. The meeting should be low-key. The purpose of the meeting (e.g., enjoyment of sports, music, fellowship, etc.) should drive the activities of the event. What are the side purposes of the event?

- To informally share the vision of the new church plant.
- To communicate the burden and passion of the ministry team members to begin a new church.
- To gather a prospect list of FRANs so they can later be contacted for future church events, or for future evangelistic contacts.

2. Suggestions to make the "Friend Day" event effective.
   - Make sure to give each guest something "valuable," for example, a New Testament, Christian book, CD, gift certificate at a Christian bookstore, and so forth.
   - Door prize drawing. (Two tickets for the member and a friend to attend another sports or musical event.)
   - A certificate for each guest for a future prize. But the friend must return to the next event sponsored by the new church for the guest to receive the prize, for example, free round of golf, pass for ladies to get fingernails fixed, free tickets for children's event.

8

Building a People-Loving Ministry

The Church at Thessalonica

Paul, Silas, and Timothy left Philippi and continued southwest along the Egnation Way until they came to the city of Thessalonica. It was the prominent city in the region. King Cassander in 315 B.C. named the city in honor of his wife, Thessalonica. It rapidly grew in both size and wealth and for a time served as the headquarters of the Macedonian navy. Even after the fall of the Greek Empire, Thessalonica remained an important trading center in the Roman Empire and continued to prosper.

A large Jewish population existed in Thessalonica, so Paul and his team returned to the practice of preaching in the synagogue. For three consecutive Sabbaths, Paul reasoned from the Scriptures "explaining and demonstrating that Christ had to suffer and rise again from the dead, and saying, 'This Jesus whom I preach to you is the Christ'" (Acts 17:3). Beginning in the synagogue yielded results, and a number were converted, including a large group of Greeks and number of prominent women in the city.

But although many believed, some Jews rejected Paul's message. They organized a riot in the marketplace. The mob attacked Jason's home where they thought the missionary team was staying. When the mob could not find them, they seized Jason and some of the others, then took them to the city officials. They were accused of harboring "these who have turned the world upside down" (v. 6) and of being involved in a movement that taught the existence of "another king—Jesus" (v. 7). When these charges were made, the officials required Jason and other Christians who had to be seized with him to post a security bond before being released. This bond apparently guaranteed that the Christians would not cause a riot and that Paul would leave the city. Although Paul agreed to leave, he later regretted it when he realized the bond also prevented him from returning to the city to visit the newly established church (1 Thess. 2:18).

Now, the Rest of the Story

The Book of Acts primarily describes the preaching ministry of Paul in the synagogue. It was only natural for the author Luke to think this was the key to success in Thessalonica, because he had seen how God effectively used Paul's preaching in the synagogues in other cities. No doubt, the synagogue ministry was important. Paul understood "it pleased God through the foolishness of the message preached to save those who believe" (1 Cor. 1:21). But in Paul's own recounting of the ministry in Thessalonica, it is evident that much more than three weeks of preaching took place.

Most Bible teachers agree Paul and his team may have remained in Thessalonica for several months. On at least two occasions during his Thessalonian ministry, Paul received a generous offering from the church in Philippi (Phil. 4:16). Despite this, Paul still found it necessary to work "night and day" so as to avoid any expense to the new church being planted (1 Thess. 2:9). All this suggests an extended stay in Thessalonica.

That extended ministry in Thessalonica probably preceded the synagogue ministry. As a stranger in town still suffering from the beating he had in Philippi, it is unlikely Paul began his synagogue ministry immediately. Even his appearance in the synagogue when he first arrived may have raised questions he did not want to answer immediately. Paul worked to cover his expenses, and it was probably here he began building relationships with others in the city. Indeed, Paul's work at building *redemptive relationships* was probably what gave his preaching credibility.

Paul's behavior in Thessalonica convinced others he had no ulterior motive in ministry (1 Thess. 2:3). It was clear he was making no effort to impress others with flattery (v. 5) or looking for any special recognition from others (v. 6). Rather, words like "gentleness" and "affectionately" best describe how Paul related to the people he met. Others recognized the similarity between his actions and those of "a nursing mother" toward "her own children" (v. 7). Indeed, the team found themselves imparting to new believers "our own lives, because you had become dear to us" (v. 8).

Paul's description of his ministry in Thessalonica makes clear he never abandoned his primary purpose of communicating the gospel to those who needed to hear it. He preached the gospel but did it in a way that others could see by his lifestyle something of the power and importance of the gospel message. While the message of the gospel is the story of God's love for people, it also tells people they have a sin problem that needs to be resolved. Because Paul had been building a *people-loving* ministry, when he confronted them with that part of the gospel, they recognized he was confronting and charging them much "as a father does his own children" (v. 11).

In the culture of the first century, concepts like *unconditional love* were foreign to most people, especially that kind of love coming from one of the gods. That idea is still hard to understand for many people today. But as the love of Christ was poured out through Paul to others, they saw something so unique they could not ignore it. Then, when he began to tell them that God's love demonstrated the gospel, they knew exactly what he was talking about. They had seen it modeled in Paul.

Using a Love Magnet to Reach People

One of D. L. Moody's biographers captured the essence of Moody's message and ministry with the title *Love Them In*. Just as honey catches more flies than vinegar, Moody understood people would be attracted to a people-loving ministry that introduced people to a people-loving God. Very early in his ministry, Moody used a love magnet to draw children to his Sunday School. When a newspaper reporter asked a young boy why he traveled across the city to attend Moody's Sunday School instead of attending one closer to his home, the boy simply responded, "They sure know how to love a fella over there."

Today, church growth authorities understand people go to the churches where they are wanted and appreciated. Church growth research suggests if church members do not begin building relationships with visitors and new converts, the newcomers will drop out. In contrast, people with as few as six or seven good friends in a church almost never leave, apart from a move to another city. Even then, they may still feel as if the old church is home for years to come.

Most churches consider themselves a friendly church because church members feel the warmth and friendship of others in the church family. It is not uncommon to see groups of people gathered throughout the church facility before and after services talking and laughing together. But often the warmth of Christian fellowship is turned inward to others in the church family and seldom experienced by outsiders who visit the congregation. Churches who want to use a love magnet to reach people should understand the need to deliberately communicate their love to people in a way that convinces them that the new church is a caring place. Simply writing "the friendliest church in the community" on the church sign or printing it in the church bulletin is usually not enough.

Growing churches understand the *Law of Three Hearings.* This law states the average visitor must attend church and listen to the gospel three or four times before he or she is comfortable enough to make a personal commitment. When someone visits your church, the immediate goal is to convince him or her to return next week. They will probably make a "bondable decision" to either accept Christ or join the church after they have attended three or four weeks.

The *Law of Seven Touches* indicates people tend to make

that second visit when they have had positive contact with at least seven people or they have been contacted seven different ways. Seven contacts can be a difficult goal to reach. Often, visitors are the last people to arrive for a church service and the first to leave. If a church is not prepared with a proactive approach toward visitors, it will be difficult to even learn the visitor's name.

Many churches designate greeters to help overcome this problem. When arriving for a service, a person may be met by a greeter in the parking lot. The greeter then walks the person in and introduces a second greeter at the door. That greeter can help the visitor find the way around the building. As the visitor enters the auditorium, he or she should be met by an usher who helps to find a seat. Before taking a seat in the auditorium, the visitor has already met two or three people in the church. Visitors form an opinion about the church through relationships. A letter from the pastor thanking the visitor for attending and inviting him or her back next week should have a personal element: a call from the church office to offer a friendship package or a visit by a member of the church visitation team to deliver that friendship package, or a call from a Bible study group leader inviting the visitor to join their Bible study group. Any one of these seven touches can make a visitor feel comfortable enough to return.

Loving people is not enough to effectively reach people with the gospel. You may love them, but they may not know it. Those you love must recognize your concern. When that happens, the love magnet can draw people into the church. The next step in helping visitors form a personal relationship with Christ often involves our building *redemptive relationships with them.*

Building Redemptive Relationships

The idea of *redemptive relationships* was a part of the social fabric of Old Testament Israel. Under the law, a relative could "redeem" a person and his property by paying his debt (Lev. 25:47-55). This custom was the basis of the romance between

Boaz and Ruth and is often considered a type of the redemptive work of Jesus Christ. The idea of establishing *redemptive relationships* may also be applied to Christians. Individuals with a natural love and concern for others can use relationships to communicate God's greater love and concern to their friends.

The story of Ruth and Boaz illustrates three primary bridge-building principles that can result in *redemptive relationships*. First, Boaz took notice of Ruth and was interested enough to learn more about her when he saw her in his field (2:5, 11). Then he repeatedly expressed his interest in her through various direct and indirect acts of kindness (vv. 8-9, 14-16). Finally, although a relationship was quickly established and recognized, he was willing to give it time to develop until Ruth herself wanted to make their relationship a means of her redemption (2:23; 3:9).

Using these same three principles, you can begin building bridges with people in your personal sphere of influence. A first step is to list all persons by name and add them to your prayer list. As stressed in previous chapters, it is always best to talk to God about people before talking to people about God. As you begin praying for those in your personal sphere of influence, ask yourself how well you know these people. You know their name, but what about their birthday, anniversary, the name of their spouse and children, personal interests and hobbies? As you ask these questions, this may motivate you to get to know some of these people better.

The key to developing meaningful relationships involves repeated *random acts of kindness* that communicate your interest in them. This may be as simple as sending a birthday card or having your friend over for a barbecue. The specific acts of kindness you do will depend on who you are reaching out to. A businessman wanted to begin building *redemptive relationships* in the office by bringing a dozen doughnuts to work, but when he arrived he learned most of his coworkers were on a diet trying to lose weight. He changed his strategy and began playing basketball after work with several colleagues.

The strongest bridges take time to build right. Don't be

surprised if your initial effort to reach out to others is met with skepticism or suspicion. Building bridges to eternity will take earthly time. As you consistently express God's love for people through *random acts of kindness,* you will be giving credibility to your witness and providing your friends with a frame of reference for understanding the unconditional love of God. Keep on keeping on, "for in due season we shall reap if we do not lose heart" (Gal. 6:9).

Barriers to Building Healthy Relationships

The whole idea of developing *redemptive relationships* sounds good, but for many people, building any kind of healthy relationship is a challenge. It seems the harder some try, the worse their relationships turn out. They want to make their marriage work, but it is not easy. They know things should be better at the office, but they just can't seem to connect with others. At the very core of their being, they long to have just one really close friend, but they have almost abandoned hope.

The Scriptures have a lot to say about building healthy relationships. Various healthy and dysfunctional relationships are described in both the Old and New Testaments. Many people find help by considering the principles emphasized in Proverbs.

In many cases, people have problems building healthy relationships because of what they learned over many years. The child who was abused by a parent often struggles later to relate to his or her children. A boy who watches his father beat his mother knows something is wrong and never learns how to treat women properly or to develop a healthy relationship with a wife. If you are struggling with the pain of your past, you may find it especially difficult to make the kind of changes you need to make to build healthy relationships. You may not even be sure that kind of change is possible. It is, but you may not be able to do it by yourself.

Talking to someone about your personal history is probably not something you are eager to do, but it may be necessary to get on with living the life you have always wanted. Still, you want to be careful about who you talk to. If you are ready to deal with the pain of your past and move on to begin building healthy relationships, make an appointment to talk with your pastor. In some cases, he may agree to work with you or network you to others in the church who can help you work through this process. In other cases, he may know someone he feels is better qualified to deal with your situation and refer you elsewhere.

The process of recovery is often challenging, even for those who want to change and become healthy. Often, that challenge prevents people from seeking the help they need. Don't let that be your story. The sooner you begin the process of recovery, the sooner you can exchange an unhealthy history for a healthy future.

How to Love the Hard-to-Love Person

Admittedly, it is easier to build relationships with some people than with others. Some personality types may especially appeal to you. They seem so warm and inviting you just can't help but want to be their friends. It seems that the more you talk, the more you find you have in common. You have heard others talk about "soul mates" and "matches made in heaven," but until you met that person, you really were not sure that was possible.

Then there are others. You know the type. Even as you read these words, certain names come to mind. You can feel yourself cringe at the very thought of being near them. It is hard to believe anyone could get under your skin as they can. Even now, if you could have things your way, you would see them as little as possible. But the real problem is that you may work with them. Worse yet, you may live with them.

Christianity is more than doctrine, it's relational. At the very core of our faith is the belief that God wants a relationship with us. That relationship grows out of His unconditional love for us. "God demonstrates His own love toward us, in that while we were still sinners, Christ died for us" (Rom.

5:8). If God loved us while we were still His enemies, it is not surprising that He expects us to love our "enemies" (Luke 6:27). That includes that hard-to-love person God may want to reach through you.

Before writing off that command as impossible, you may want to take a closer look at Jesus' instructions to His disciples. He didn't just tell them to love their enemies. He went on to tell them how to love their enemies. His advice may be just what you need to develop a *redemptive relationship* with the hard-to-love people in your life.

He began by telling His disciples to "do good to those who hate you" (Luke 6:27). Dismantle the wall of hate around others with *random acts of kindness.* Then, "bless those who curse you" (v. 28*a*). When you hear someone has been saying bad things about you, think of something really nice to say about them. You can be sure that will get back to your hard-to-love friend in a hurry. Then, "pray for those who spitefully use you" (v. 28*b*). *Random acts of kindness* and making positive comments about negative people will go a long way toward building relationships. When you pray about a bad relationship, you invite God to intervene on your behalf. That's a pretty good idea. After all, who knows more about loving hard-to-love people than God?

Building a healthy relationship with a hard-to-love person often takes time and is not easy. In the context of talking about loving our enemies, Jesus also spoke about turning the other cheek (v. 29), knowing that it is likely to cost you (v. 30). Treat people the way you want them to treat you, even when they aren't treating you right (v. 31). When it comes right down to it, loving hard-to-love people involves modeling God's love toward us (v. 35). "Therefore, be merciful, just as your Father also is merciful" (v. 36).

Personal Lessons to Take Away

1. I need to reach out to make friends with visitors who are attending my church.

2. I can reach people for Christ through *redemptive relationships*.

3. I can be used of God through involvement with others.

4. I can help a new church get started by helping to contact visitors or potential friends to a new church.

5. I can learn to love hard-to-love individuals.

6. I can overcome relationship difficulties by the peace of God and with help from other believers.

Church Lessons to Take Away

1. We must get visitors to attend our church more than one time if we expect them to make a commitment to our church.

2. We must reach out to touch visitors several times if we expect them to return to our church or to make a commitment for membership or salvation.

3. We must organize so our members are in a place to form *redemptive relationships* that will draw visitors to Christ and the church.

4. Our church must organize intentional plans to touch all visitors several times.

5. We must teach our members how to love "the hard-to-love people."

Personal Projects

Part of the success of Paul's ministry in Thessalonica must be attributed to his commitment to building *redemptive relationships* in the context of a people-loving ministry. What about you? How does God want you to get involved in the people-loving outreach of your church? It is time once again to put the Book of Acts into action.

1. Do you have problems building healthy relationships with others? That problem is not as uncommon as you may think. Identify challenges that may hinder you from building

a meaningful relationship with others. In some cases, you may need to talk with your pastor or a Christian counselor to deal with baggage you are carrying from past relationships.

2. Are you using "the love magnet" to reach people for Christ? As you look over those in your personal sphere of influence, how well do you know them? What *random act of kindness* could you do for them this week that would demonstrate your concern for them? As you review the section *Building Redemptive Relationships,* consider ways you can develop your relationships to effectively reach people for Christ.

3. Develop a prayer list of names that make you cringe even as you mention them in prayer. It is hard to hug a porcupine, and some people can only be described as "hard-to-love." If you have someone like that on your prayer list, review the section *How to Love the Hard-to-Love Person* to help you find ways you can express God's love toward them. Don't be surprised if it takes time to convince them of your sincerity. Just keep on loving them just as Christ keeps on loving you.

Church Project

As we plan and target a neighborhood to begin a new church, we must begin preparing the church planting team to relate and bond with new people in the new neighborhood where we will be ministering.

1. Make a list of those in the new neighborhood that are already in the present church, or those who have some relationship or acquaintance with those in the present church.

2. Target these people for special prayer.

3. Plan a nonchurch activity that will give you opportunity to meet new people in the neighborhood or form relationships with them, for example, cookouts, dinners, pool parties, take a gang to a sports activity, invite them to attend community activities together, and so forth.

4. Create a list of potential "friends." Invite them to present church activities that have broad public appeal, picnics,

sports events, Bible conferences, banquets, musical events, and so forth.

5. Contact these friends by E-mail, phone, letters, visits, and so forth.

6. Plan a personal outreach month when each member of a church planting team takes a new "friend" to lunch, coffee, dinner, a sports event, or an evening entertainment.

9
Building a Bible-Based Ministry

The Berean Church

The continued opposition by the Jews against Paul did not stop him from preaching. Forced to leave Thessalonica, Paul traveled west to the city of Berea. Here, Paul found people willing to give careful consideration to his message. Luke describes the Bereans as "more fair-minded than those in Thessalonica, in that they received the word with all readiness, and searched the Scriptures daily to find out whether these things were so" (Acts 17:11).

The preaching of the gospel to a group that was open to study of the Scriptures was bound to have a significant response. As a result of the Bible-teaching ministry of Paul, "many of them believed, and also not a few of the Greeks, prominent women as well as men" (v. 12). Those converted in Berea came to faith in Christ through the careful study of the Scripture. As a result, more here than in other places, the Berean Christians had a strong faith grounded in the Word of God. Even today, many churches, Bible colleges, and Bible study groups use "Berean" in their name because of their commitment to studying the Bible.

Although Paul had a successful ministry in Berea, his adversaries from Thessalonica were not content to allow his ministry to prosper. When they "learned that the word of God was preached by Paul at Berea, they came there also and stirred up the crowds" (v. 13). Paul realized the opposition was directed primarily at him. He knew his continued presence in that community would sooner or later make the Berean Christians themselves targets of persecution. The Bereans were still interested in studying the Scriptures and continued to grow in their newfound faith. Paul faced a difficult choice. If he stayed in Berea, he could help them continue to grow as Christians, but he might also make them targets of persecution. If he left, the Christians might be safe, but he would no longer be able to teach such eager students of the Word.

To resolve the problem, Paul chose to leave Berea and travel to Athens. Perhaps Paul concluded that his leaving would cause those who had come to stir up problems to follow him to Athens. Athens was a long way from Berea. Another option was that the troublemakers might return to Thessalonica with Paul's departure, celebrating their success in driving Paul out of Macedonia. In either case, the church at Berea would be spared. Paul had complete confidence in his two associates, Silas and Timothy, so he made his trip to Athens alone and left Silas and Timothy to continue developing a Bible-based ministry in Berea.

Paul's ministry in Berea was consistent with his ministry in other communities. He usually went to the synagogue to teach the Scriptures in an effort to explain that Jesus was the Messiah. The difference in Berea was he was able to develop that ministry further because of the receptivity of the Bereans. Starting a new church out of a home Bible study is used by many church planting agencies to help insure a new church will have a Bible-based ministry.

The City of Berea

The Roman senator Cicero once described the city of Berea as being "out of the way." It was a town in the district of Emathia, in southwestern Macedonia. It was located at the foot of Mount Bermius on the tributary of the Haliacmon River. By the time Paul and his team arrived in Berea, the town had been around for over 300 years. During that time, it had earned the distinction of being the first Macedonian city to surrender to Rome.

When the apostles arrived, there was much about the city itself that may have suggested their visit would be marked by tranquillity. Looking toward the southern horizon, they could see the snowcapped peak of Mount Olympus. Berea was far enough inland that life tended to move at a slower pace than in the busier coastal city. It was the kind of city that attracted people. As a result, this quiet, out-of-the-way city was one of the largest cities in the region.

One group in particular who had been attracted to Berea were the Jews. Though scattered throughout the Roman Empire, the Jews maintained their commitment to monotheism and found offensive Rome's insistence upon emperor worship. While emperor worship was the law of the land, it tended to be enforced more often in seats of Roman authority and less often elsewhere. In Berea, the Jews were free to worship God in the synagogue with limited interference. As long as they kept the peace in Berea, there would be no pressure on the Jews to prove their loyalty to Rome with a sacrifice to Caesar.

When Paul arrived, he followed his usual custom of preaching in the synagogue. His message of the gospel was not simply an account of recent events. Rather, Paul's sermons had deep roots in the Old Testament. He had studied the law thoroughly as a Pharisee, but it was not until he trusted Christ as Savior that he understood its real message. When he found a group eager to study the Scriptures, he was even more eager to teach. It is not surprising that people not only came to faith in Christ in Berea but also experienced significant spiritual growth.

The Value of Personal Bible Study

Spiritual growth is just one value you get from personal Bible study (1 Pet. 2:2). Paul told the Corinthian Christians the study of the Scriptures was a key to the growth of Christian character (1 Cor. 3:2). He also linked personal Bible study with growing faith (Rom. 10:17). In His Upper Room Discourse, Jesus linked abiding in the Scriptures with answered prayer (John 15:5). In His high-priestly prayer, Jesus linked sanctification to the Word of God (17:17). It is no wonder, then, that Paul often commended churches "to God and to the word of His grace, which is able to build you up" (Acts 20:32).

How to Understand the Bible

Many Christians today struggle with the idea of a regular consistent Bible study. Unlike the Bereans, they are content to take the views expressed by their pastor or Bible teacher. As a result, they seldom study the Bible for themselves. Some who do venture to study the Bible depend heavily on commentaries and other Bible study books to help them understand the Scriptures. While God places pastors and Bible teachers in churches to help people understand His message, and Bible commentaries and study books have their place, nothing beats personally getting into the Scriptures to discover its truths.

Paul himself recognized some people have difficulty understanding the Scriptures. He reminded the Corinthians, "But the natural man does not receive the things of the Spirit of God, for they are foolishness to him; nor can he know them, because they are spiritually discerned" (1 Cor. 2:14). Because the Bible was inspired by the Holy Spirit and is a spiritual book, we cannot adequately understand it without the Holy Spirit. One of the reasons God has given Christians the indwelling presence of the Holy Spirit is to help them comprehend the Scriptures. According to Paul, "Now we have received, not the spirit of the world, but the Spirit who is from God, that we might know the things that have been freely given to us by God" (v. 12).

Bible teachers call this ministry of the Holy Spirit "illumination." Illumination is the ministry of the Holy Spirit that enables us to understand and apply the spiritual message of the Scriptures. Before you sit before an open Bible to begin discovery of Scripture, ask the Holy Spirit to enable you to understand the Scriptures. Christians who do this often begin their Bible study with David's prayer, "Open my eyes, that I may see wondrous things from Your law" (Ps. 119:18).

Simply praying David's prayer does not ensure one will have a complete understanding of the Scriptures. An individual will hinder the work of the Holy Spirit when that person allows sin into his or her life. That's why Paul prayed for the

Colossians, "That you may walk worthy of the Lord, fully pleasing Him, being fruitful in every good work and increasing in the knowledge of God" (1:10). There is a relationship between wanting to study the Scriptures and understanding them more completely.

Some Christians take a very mystical approach to the Scriptures and tend to make them say all kinds of things that later hinder their spiritual growth. This problem can be avoided if we interpret the Bible as we might interpret any literary work. You must follow the normal rules of grammar to understand the meaning of the Bible. Conservative Bible teachers call this the historical-grammatical interpretation of the Bible.

When we interpret a passage of Scripture, we should keep the historical context in mind. Since the author spoke to a historical setting, understanding something about that background will help us interpret the text. Also, the more we know about the human author, the easier it will be to understand what he was trying to say in the original context.

As we consider the context, we ought also to consider the grammatical context. Words are important as vehicles of thought in the inspired text. A good rule to follow in Bible study has been expressed as follows: "When the plain sense makes sense, seek no other sense."

While much of the Scriptures is clear in meaning, the biblical authors also used figurative language, including metaphors, similes, and parables. When this language is used in Scripture, the immediate context usually makes it clear what the author was trying to emphasize. Sometimes, you may need an understanding of other parts of the Scriptures to understand some symbols. When John the Baptist called Jesus "the Lamb of God who takes away the sin of the world" (John 1:29), that metaphor is best understood in the context of the Old Testament use of a sacrificial lamb for the sin offering.

Personal Lessons to Take Away

1. I must learn the content and principles of the Word of God if I am going to be a well-rounded Christian.

2. I must know and apply the Bible principles for church life to be a mature functioning member of a local church that is growing.

3. I need to be strong in Bible teaching if I expect my church to be a strong Bible church.

Church Lessons to Take Away

1. A church cannot be rightly planted if the new members do not have a firm understanding of Bible content, its personal application, and the biblical principles necessary for a healthy church to operate.

2. Church planters must base their preaching and teaching on the Word of God.

3. For new members to grow in Christ, they must be taught the content and principles of God's Word.

Personal Projects

If God gave the Bible to change your life, then it is reasonable to ask, "How will your life be changed?" It is time once again to put the Book of Acts into action. As you consider the following suggestions, choose one that will best help you apply what God has been teaching you about building a Bible-based ministry.

1. A Bible-based ministry grows out of a life committed to personal Bible study. Research suggests many Christians fail to read their Bibles outside of a church service. Perhaps that is because they fail to recognize the value of personal Bible study. Identify any attitudes you may have that hinder you from personal Bible study. If you are not reading the Bible daily, set a goal to read through the Book of Proverbs this month, one chapter each day. List the insights you gain as you read each chapter. By the end of the month, you will have your own reasons to be involved in personal Bible study.

2. If you do read the Scriptures daily, perhaps it is time to move on to the next step. Follow the suggestions in the section *How to Understand the Bible* to guide the study of a Bible book. As you discover new insights, be sure to share them

with others so that they, too, might benefit from your personal Bible study.

3. As you study the Scriptures, do you find yourself getting excited about what you discover? Then maybe it is time for you to consider preparing to lead a Bible study group. The idea may be a little scary at first, but God often calls people to a specific ministry by first giving them the desire to do it (1 Tim. 3:1). Talk to your pastor about becoming better equipped to lead a Bible study group in your church or the target neighborhood where your church plans to start a new church.

Church Projects

1. *Vision Statement and/or Ministry Statement.* The new church you plant should purpose to both teach and preach the Bible (Acts 5:42). Is this purpose included in the new church's statement of ministry or vision? Revise your statement. Does it say how you want the new church to minister? Especially in light of the strengths of the Berean Church, what do you want the new church plant to do about teaching the Bible?

2. *Sunday School/Bible Study.* From the very beginning, plan to organize a program of weekly Bible study that is:

- *Complete:* that is, it covers the Bible from Genesis to Revelation.
- *Comprehensive:* that is, it studies the Bible by survey, history, biography, doctrine, topic, prophecy, devotional study, and so forth.
- *Practical:* that is, it applies the Bible to the total life and attitude of the members.
- *Age-Graded:* that is, it includes Bible study by all ages, offered at the understanding level of each person in the church.
- *Professional and Lay Taught:* The pastor should be equipped to teach the Bible to all persons in the church, as well as a lay program where laypeople are taught how to teach the Bible, then recruited into a program to do so.

10 Presenting the Gospel to the Secular Mind

The Church at Athens

Paul's ministry in Greece focused in the two principal cities of that province, Athens and Corinth. These two cities were different in many ways, and that difference impacted Paul's ministry style. The way Paul explained the gospel to an Athenian philosopher was different from the way he explained it to a sailor passing through Corinth. The message always remained the same, but Paul used many different methods of communicating the gospel. On every occasion, he communicated the death, burial, and resurrection of Jesus as the heart of the gospel (1 Cor. 15:3-4).

The city of Athens had already existed for over a thousand years before Paul traveled from the harbor into the center of the city. Over the years, Athens had become a center of Greek sciences and arts. During the Roman era, Athens became one of the respected intellectual centers of the empire. Also as a strongly religious center, Athens was home to a number of temples, altars, and statues to Greek gods and goddesses including Zeus (Jupiter) and Athena. There was even an altar devoted to the worship of "The Unknown God" (Acts 17:23).

As Paul waited for the arrival of his team, he became increasingly concerned about the widespread idolatry he witnessed. Soon he found himself again involved in the task of preaching the gospel to those who had not yet heard and responded to Christ. In Athens, Paul adopted a twofold strategy to reach the people. First, because there was a sizable Jewish population in the town, Paul followed his usual strategy; he "reasoned in the synagogue with the Jews and with the Gentile worshipers" (v. 17). Second, because the city was essentially Greek in its population, Paul adopted the Greek approach by raising questions and discussing issues in the marketplace.

The Greeks prided themselves on their democratic tolerance of new ideas and pluralism. It was common for teachers and philosophers to gather in public places to discuss their ideas. In a city like Athens, anyone could speak in the marketplace provided they had something to say and did not mind being challenged by others who had a different perspective on the issue.

Many people gathered in the Athenian market and the Areopagus (Mars Hill) who "spent their time in nothing else but either to tell or to hear some new thing" (v. 21). Some of the Epicurean and Stoic philosophers who met Paul in the market wondered what he was teaching. They were told by others, "He seems to be a proclaimer of foreign gods" (v. 18).

As curiosity about Paul's message grew, Paul was invited to address the Athenians in the more formal setting of the Areopagus. Paul accepted this opportunity to address the group and preached a sermon that some modern-day scholars have criticized for its lack of biblical content. Unlike the other sermons Paul preached in the Jewish synagogues, this address to the philosophers on Mars Hill makes no reference to the Old Testament Scriptures or the Messiah. At one point Paul even quoted a pagan poet.

In Paul's preaching, he constantly sought to build bridges with his listeners and bring them around to his conclusion. When talking to those who knew the Scriptures, Paul appealed to the Scriptures. But it is doubtful this crowd was familiar with the Scriptures or that appealing to them would have established any credibility in their mind. Instead, Paul used sources with which the people were familiar.

Those who are especially critical of Paul's sermon often claim he changed his message and therefore got no results. Neither of these claims is consistent with the biblical account or the transcription of the sermon. Paul clearly identified God as the One "who made the world and everything in it" in contrast to the Athenian view of many gods. Paul also spoke directly against the practice of idolatry so common in that city (vv. 24, 29). Also included in Paul's message was a clear call to repentance and affirmation of the resurrection of Jesus (vv. 30-31). The message was so clear and comprehensive that Paul was interrupted by heckling, rather than an attempt by them to challenge or change Paul's content. However, while the bulk of popular opinion appears to have rejected the gospel on this occasion, "some men joined him and believed, among them Dionysius the Areopagite, a woman named Damaris, and others with them" (v. 34).

Preaching the Gospel in a Hostile World

Everybody is reachable, but some people are harder to reach than others. They turn down invitations to attend church with you and change topics when you begin sharing the gospel. Some may even express hostile attitudes toward the church, its members, and its message. Others simply appear apathetic or uninterested. While they demonstrate their resistance to the gospel in different ways, they may just simply be hard-to-reach people. You may have someone like that on your prayer list, someone whose personal experience, involvement with a religious cult, or history of bad experiences with a Christian or church puts up seemingly insurmountable barriers to the gospel.

Paul himself struggled with the tension between the ease of reaching receptive people in the synagogue and trying to reach the hard-to-reach secular people. During his ministry in Corinth, he was largely rejected by the Jews and welcomed by the Gentiles of that city (Acts 18:6-10). Yet while in Corinth he wrote an Epistle to the Romans that expressed his deep burden for his people the Jews (Rom. 9:1-3; 10:1).

When Jesus died for our sins, He died "for the whole world" (1 John 2:2). This means He has already provided the means by which the hard-to-reach person can be saved. If He has provided for their salvation, it is reasonable to conclude He wants even hard-to-reach people saved (1 Tim. 2:4; 2 Pet.

3:9). Ultimately, it is God who makes people responsive to the gospel.

While making people receptive to the gospel is the work of God, He uses means to accomplish this work. Church growth researchers conclude people tend to be more receptive to the gospel during periods of sociological disorientation in their life. This is why major changes in society such as war, liberation, famine, or other natural disaster often result in a period of significant revival or church growth immediately after the emergency. But the same principle may be applied on a personal level. When people experience a major change in their personal life, such as the death of a friend or family member, marriage, birth of a child, career change, or divorce, they tend to be more open to the gospel than at other times. Therefore, we should be sensitive to the changes in our friend's life that may change his or her receptivity to the gospel.

All this can be a little intimidating at times. When the pastor of a church encouraged his people to be part of a special week of visitation in their community, some older Christians were initially reluctant to join the effort. They recalled efforts 30 years earlier when the community was strongly opposed to the starting of an Evangelical church. After much prayer, the older Christians decided to join the effort, not because they thought it would work, but because they wanted to encourage their pastor. They were surprised as they knocked on doors to share the gospel to find a warm reception. The community had changed over the decades, so much that the church leaders concluded God had intervened because of the hours of prayer that had been devoted to reaching that area. Prayer still changes things, even in a world that is hostile to the gospel.

Building Bridges While Maintaining Fences

A strong resistance to the gospel is usually an indication of internal barriers to the gospel. In most cases, a person will not respond to the gospel until that barrier has been removed. Dr. Donald A. McGavran, the father of the church growth movement, noted, "People like to become Christians without crossing racial, linguistic, or class barriers." Just as a truck driver takes the longer highway around a city rather than the shorter route through the heart of the city to avoid stop-and-go traffic, so people like to come to Christ in a way that involves the least discomfort.

If barriers are the difference between the hard-to-reach person and the receptive person, then removing barriers needs to be your major strategy. Since there is nothing particularly pious or spiritual in forcing people to jump hurdles, let's get rid of them. Making people jump hurdles is totally contrary to the apostolic method (1 Cor. 9:19-23). Those who don't work to remove barriers may unwittingly be guilty of adding to the biblical conditions of salvation, something no discerning Christian would want to do (Rev. 22:18).

INTERNAL BARRIERS TO WITNESSING

1. The message, that is, the gospel
2. The necessity of belief and repentance
3. The rejection of good works for salvation

While removing barriers is important in evangelism, it is also important to keep some barriers in place. At the very heart of the gospel are certain barriers that cannot be removed without radically changing the gospel itself. If we develop a marketing strategy to make it easy to join the church or become a Christian, we might water down the gospel and make it less than Christianity. Remember, evangelism is more than marketing. The gospel that sells is not the gospel that saves.

Historically, Evangelical Christians have always believed that certain essential principles remain nonnegotiable. These include (1) the divine inspiration of the Scriptures, the source of our knowledge of the gospel, (2) the virgin birth of Christ, which also implies His sinless character and deity, (3) the vicarious atonement of Christ on the Cross, that is, that Christ died for our sins and that His death is sufficient to save, (4) the victorious resurrection of Christ on the third day to give us eternal life, and (5) the visible return of Christ for His own. It is doubtful if one can intelligently deny the biblical teaching of these essentials and be considered a Christian.

In addition to these foundational beliefs, there is the repentance aspect of the gospel that many people see as a barrier to becoming a Christian. This second barrier is essential to the message of the Cross. Paul affirmed, "We preach Christ crucified, to the Jews a stumbling block and to the Greeks foolishness" (1 Cor. 1:23). In Athens, he was openly ridiculed for expressing his belief in the resurrection from the dead (Acts 17:32), yet that doctrine calls for the listener to believe, repent, and follow Jesus Christ (23:6; 24:21; 26:23).

A third barrier that can never be removed is our view of good works. Some people consider a "grace only" view of salvation as inadequate. The natural person wants to do something to gain merit before God. Salvation is accomplished by the grace of God alone, "not of works, lest anyone should boast" (Eph. 2:9).

EXTERNAL BARRIERS

1. E-0 Internal Barrier
2. E-1 Stained-Glass Barrier
3. E-2 Cultural and Class Barrier
4. E-3 Linguistic Barrier

The first is *E-0 Barrier,* which is dealing with people already in the church, that is, unsaved church members who were born into the church or transferred their membership but were never born again. It is sometimes hard to witness to unsaved church members because they are spiritually blinded to the gospel (2 Cor. 4:3-4) or they have heard the gospel and hardened their hearts.

The second, the *E-1 Barrier,* is usually a negative statement about the church building or negative feelings from an unsaved person about your church. This person says the pews are hard, the gospel invitation is too long, the building is too old or cold, or they don't like meeting in temporary facilities. Sometimes your church's name is an E-1 Barrier.

The third, the *E-2 Barrier,* means they have different cultural habits or dress from the Christians in your church. They feel uncomfortable in your church because they are the only ones with their racial characteristics in your church. Sometimes the rich are uncomfortable with the poor, or vice versa.

The fourth barrier is the *E-3 Barrier.* This used to be the problem of the foreign missionary, but more and more we find people with different languages or dialects in North America.

EXTERNAL BARRIERS

1. E-0 INTERNAL BARRIER
Overcoming the barriers of those unsaved in the church, for example, spiritual blindness, hardness to the gospel, ignorance of the gospel, and so forth.

2. E-1 STAINED-GLASS BARRIER
Overcoming the barriers of people in the church's neighborhood, for example poor location, comfort in the building, cleanliness, type of building, wrong type of denomination, and so forth.

3. E-2 CULTURAL AND CLASS BARRIER
Witnessing to people of a different ethnic, race, or socioeconomic background.

4. E-3 LINGUISTIC BARRIER
Witnessing to people who speak a different dialect or language.

While it is important to maintain God's fences to preserve the integrity of the gospel, bridges can overcome human barriers to the gospel. These human barriers tend to be cultural. Understanding fences and barriers will not only ensure that the gospel is clear but also guarantee that the gospel is clearly understood.

What You Need to Know About the Gospel

God's plan of salvation is simple. First, people need to know they are lost. "For all have sinned and fall short of the glory of God" (Rom. 3:23). Second, they need to know the penalty for their sin. "The wages of sin is death" (6:23). Third, they need to know about God's provision for their sin. "While we were still sinners, Christ died for us" (5:8). But simply knowing these things is not enough. People become Christians when they believe the gospel (10:9) and receive Christ as Savior by faith (John 1:12).

Some people have honest questions about the gospel that need to be answered before they can respond. In many cases, when these questions are addressed, they will feel more comfortable trusting Christ for their salvation. When the disciples told Thomas that Jesus was risen, Thomas had a hard time believing what he was hearing. A week later, Jesus met with His disciples again. It appears Jesus' primary purpose in that second visit was to address Thomas's concerns so he, too, could believe (20:24-29).

A college student told a campus evangelist he had an intellectual problem with Christianity. The evangelist told the student he was almost right. "You're only off by 18 inches," he claimed. "Your problem is not in your head, it is in your heart. You may understand the gospel, but you just don't want to respond." Jesus told the Jewish leaders of His day they had the same problem. It was not that they did not understand what He taught, they simply refused His message because of their sin. Not everyone who has questions about God really wants answers.

For many years, C. S. Lewis would have described himself as a skeptic. He was prepared to consider Jesus as a great teacher, but that was all. After he became a Christian, he examined the teaching of Christ more carefully. When he considered Jesus' claim to be God and the only way to the Father (John 14:6), Lewis realized that trusting Jesus was a very rational thing to do. He concluded that any man who made the claims that Jesus made had to fall into one of two categories. First, He must have known He was wrong and therefore a liar, or if He believed He was right, He was therefore a lunatic. But there was a third conclusion. If the man knew who He was and told the truth, then C. S. Lewis concluded he (Lewis) had to fall to his knees and worship Him as the Lord of the Universe.

It has been said the greatest evidence for Christianity was an empty tomb outside of Jerusalem. Even today, almost two millennia after the fact, Christians from all over the world still travel to Israel to visit the Garden Tomb. There they celebrate the miracle of the Resurrection. The message of a resurrected Christ was the consistent emphasis of the apostles' preaching, a fact that no one could dispute. No one who has ever asked the question, "Who moved the stone?" and searched diligently for the answer has ever found a reason to doubt the gospel. Many who tried to explain it away became devoted Christians in the process of trying to destroy the faith.

The Greatest Defense Is a Personal Offense

The greatest defense of the gospel is the testimony of a changed life. A hostile person can challenge your rational arguments, and they can debate your logic. But they have no answer when you share your testimony of a changed life. "But sanctify the Lord God in your hearts, and always be ready to give a defense to everyone who asks you a reason for the hope that is in you, with meekness and fear" (1 Pet. 3:15).

Personal Lessons to Take Away

1. I can always share my testimony, even when I can't answer those who criticize Christianity or I can't preach an apologetic sermon.

2. I must recognize and answer internal barriers that keep unsaved people from receiving Christ.

3. I will use one method when witnessing to unsaved people from a "Christian" environment and a different method when witnessing to unsaved people from a completely secular background.

4. I must never give up my belief in the doctrinal essentials of the faith.

5. I can only bring lost people to Christ with the gospel; it will not be by my logic, my arguments, or my persuasive speech.

Church Lessons to Take Away

1. A church can be planted in a hostile community because God has prepared some in that community to respond to Christ.

2. A church can overcome barriers to its preaching by the personal testimony of its members.

3. A church must always remain committed to the essentials of Christianity.

4. A church must rely on the gospel to get people saved, not its marketing, its methods, or its persuasive means of communication.

Personal Projects

When God called Isaiah to preach, He told him he would preach to a hostile and unresponsive audience (6:9-10). Yet even then, God promised Isaiah a remnant would respond. Sometimes, we miss out on witnessing a person's conversion because we misinterpret initial hostility or apathy as evidence that the person is unreachable.

Paul didn't fail in Athens; Dionysius, Damaris, and others came to faith in Christ that day. However, Paul preached in a different *manner* in Athens, but he did not preach a different *message*. He simply used a different approach to build bridges with those he was trying to reach.

Once again let's put the Book of Acts into action. As you consider the following suggestions, choose one that will best help you apply what God has been teaching you about understanding the cultural values to reach out to people in your community.

1. Admittedly, this world is not a friend to grace. Whenever Christians begin sharing their faith with others, they are

bound to get some hostile responses. Identify any fears you may have. Ask God to replace your fear with faith to overcome the issues that intimidate you.

2. Perhaps someone on your prayer list could be described as a skeptic. It is widely believed that becoming a Christian amounts to committing intellectual suicide. If you have a friend like that, review the section *What You Need to Know About the Gospel* to help you address those concerns. If you want to pursue the topic further, check your church library or local Christian bookstore to find a good book on apologetics. Some apologetic books are designed to equip you to witness to a skeptical friend. Others are suitable to give a friend to read.

3. Can you tell someone about the change God has made in your life in less than two minutes? If not, work on developing your testimony this week. See *Church Project* and *Preparing Your Personal Testimony.* Make sure to write out your personal testimony, then you will "always be ready to give a defense to everyone who asks you a reason for the hope that is in you" (1 Pet. 3:15).

Church Project

The church project is designed to help all members of the ministry team prepare and use their "Personal Testimony" in witnessing as they attempt to plant a new church.

Preparing Your Personal Testimony

1. *Your testimony will overcome barriers.* One of the hardest things for a skeptic to deal with is the testimony of a changed life. Even when a person doesn't notice the change that has taken place in his or her life, others often do. Learning how to share your personal testimony is one way to overcome barriers and build bridges to others so they can hear and consider the gospel for themselves.

2. *Your testimony tells your life message.* Your testimony is an expression of what God has done in your life. It tells the most important thing in your life, that is, your meeting God. Normally, a testimony focuses on your conversion experience,

although it is not uncommon to also include what God has been doing in your life since your conversion. The content of your testimony depends on what you are trying to accomplish with it. If you are using your testimony in evangelism, it is best to talk about what happened at your conversion.

While it may not be necessary to know exactly when you were converted, it is absolutely necessary that you know that you were converted. First, you must personally experience salvation. When God has done something in your life, you want to tell others.

3. *Steps to prepare your testimony.* Prepare your testimony by praying for divine guidance (James 1:5-6). Ask God to help you prepare your testimony from His perspective. Let Him show you how He can use it to draw others to himself.

On three occasions the apostle Paul gave his personal testimony (Acts 22:1-21; 26:2-23; Gal. 1:13-24). In each account, Paul had a plan. He began first by briefly describing his life before his conversion. Second, he told his listeners how he was converted. Then he described the difference his conversion had made in his life. That three-point outline is a good guide for preparing your personal testimony.

Be positive. Emphasize the good things God has done for you, rather than the failings of your old life. Also, emphasize the good things you have in Christ rather than the things you lost in becoming a Christian. Whenever your life changes, there are gains and losses. But the change that took place in your conversion had far more gains than losses. Therefore, emphasize your gains and use your testimony to affirm the positive character of the Christian life.

It is often best to focus on a single theme in preparing your testimony. Describe your experience in the context of loneliness, addiction, a pursuit of happiness, or a search for personal fulfillment. Then, people with similar needs will readily identify with your experience.

As you describe your life before conversion, remember, your purpose is to build a bridge between yourself and the listener. Include enough detail to enable the other person to readily identify with your experience, but be careful not to glamorize the past experiences. Jesus described both sides of conversion when He said, "The thief does not come except to steal, and to kill, and to destroy. I have come that they may have life, and that they may have it more abundantly" (John 10:10).

The climax of your testimony should answer the question, "What does Christ mean to you today?" If you have a meaningful relationship with Christ, there are probably many ways you could answer that question. But it is best to mention only two or three things that are most significant. Emphasize what is most meaningful in your life, and try not to sound like a soap or shampoo commercial. Your testimony is an expression of what God has done in your life. It doesn't have to be exciting, but it should be interesting.

4. *Write out your testimony.* It is important to write the main part of your testimony. Take time to work on an opening statement that is likely to capture the interest of the listener and is consistent with the rest of your testimony. You may wish to include one or two significant scriptures into your testimony. Make them flow with your presentation. Be careful not to turn your testimony into a Bible lesson or sermon.

5. *Practice on one another.* Take time when the ministry team meets together to have each person share his or her testimony. It's good to have your testimony written out, but do not read them to one another. Share them with one another. As a matter of fact, allow time to have each share his or her testimony with one other person in the group.

Conclusion

As each person on the ministry team shares his or her testimony with one another, it will not only strengthen each person but also bond the team together in closer unity than ever before. It will also equip members to be witnesses in their daily lives as well as prepare them to minister in the new neighborhood where they are planting a church.

11 Building a Ministry Team That Ministers

The Corinthian Church

The seaport city of Corinth was a cosmopolitan center of people from various parts of the Roman Empire. The harbor at Corinth was one of the few located along that coast, so the city naturally became a center of trade. To save sailing all the way around the peninsula of Greece, smaller ships were transported across the isthmus between Corinth and Cenchrea over a series of wooden rails. Sailors could save three or four days on the sea, and this traffic only added to the amount of trade passing through the port of Corinth.

Because Corinth was a seaport, the city had extremely loose morals. The Greeks said immoral people "lived like a Corinthian." In his first letter to them, Paul reminded his readers that some of them had been idol worshipers, sodomites, terrorists, and extortionists prior to their conversion (1 Cor. 6:9-11).

Soon after arriving in Corinth, Paul met a man named Aquila and his wife, Priscilla. Because of the emperor's persecution of the Jews, Aquila and his wife had apparently moved their tentmaking business from Asia to Corinth. Paul was hired by the couple to make tents because he had been trained in the same occupation as a boy in Tarsus.

Although Paul was engaged in tentmaking during the week, he continued to preach in the synagogue, taking every advantage to reason with both the Jews and the Greeks about Jesus, the Messiah. While tentmaking is one means of church planting, it is probably not the only one. Denominations and other churches have supported church planters. Perhaps your church has done the same thing.

Timothy and Silas finally arrived from Macedonia. Very likely they brought with them a financial gift from the church at Philippi (Phil. 4:15). This gift made it possible for Paul to devote more of his energies to preaching the gospel and getting a church established. Paul continued his ministry in the synagogue, preaching with an even greater intensity than he had prior to the arrival of his associates.

As Paul pressed his message that Jesus was indeed the Messiah, the Jews became increasingly more resistant. Finally, Paul addressed their rejection noting, "Your blood be upon your own heads; I am clean. From now on I will go to the Gentiles" (Acts 18:6). In the Old Testament, the prophets were viewed as guilty of the blood of those who were judged unless they had made a determined effort to warn them (Ezek. 33:8-9). When the Jews in Corinth rejected Jesus as their Messiah, Paul claimed that his responsibility for preaching to them was complete, and that he was going to turn his attention from that point primarily to the Gentiles.

Paul's decision to preach to the Gentiles rather than Jews meant he no longer had access to the synagogue. He moved the Christians into the home of Justus, a Gentile who worshiped God and lived next to the synagogue. This move apparently did not hinder the effectiveness of Paul's preaching. A large group of people were converted after the move, including the household of Crispus, the ruler of the synagogue, and many of the Corinthians. Despite the continued success of his ministry, Paul probably had inner concerns about the move.

It was difficult for Paul to turn his back on his Jewish heritage. Part of that heritage taught him it was wrong to worship God in a place of one's choosing, but that God had designated the Tabernacle or Temple for worship (Deut. 12). While that applied specifically to the Temple in Jerusalem, the Jews also applied that idea to each local synagogue. Also, Paul knew from past experience that once the Jews had rejected the gospel, it would not be long before they would attack him and he would have to leave the town. Paul may have had second thoughts about leaving the synagogue.

Then the Lord appeared to him in a night vision. He was told, "Do not be afraid, but speak, and do not keep silent; for I am with you, and no one will attack you to hurt you; for I have many people in this city" (Acts 18:9-10). That meant God approved Paul's moving the church out of the synagogue into a private home.

Paul remained in Corinth for an additional 18 months after the vision, continuing to teach God's Word. As he suspected, the Jews continued directing opposition toward him. It was so intense that at one point Paul was arrested and brought before Gallio, the proconsul of Achaia. Paul was formally charged with persuading "men to worship God contrary to the law" (v. 13), but before Paul could begin his defense, the case was thrown out of court because Gallio claimed the dispute was a question of Jewish custom and that was outside his court's jurisdiction. The city officials concluded the Jews were creating this problem. So "the Greeks took Sosthenes, the ruler of the synagogue, and beat him" publicly outside the court (v. 17). When Gallio heard what was taking place in front of his own judgment hall, he chose not to take any action. Sosthenes later converted to Christianity and became a helper of Paul in ministry (1 Cor. 1:1).

Paul's Ministry Team

Long before it became a popular concept, Paul believed in and practiced a "team ministry" approach to getting the job done for Christ. He realized the task of reaching the Gentile world was too big for one man to attempt all by himself. Although Paul was a multigifted individual, even he realized there were some things others could do better. Also, because of time restraints, Paul realized some things should be delegated to others to free him to focus on those things he could do best. Therefore, it is not surprising that Paul partnered with a long list of men and women throughout his ministry.

Those on a mature team are more concerned with helping others complete a common goal than building individual reputations or looking for things to add to their personal ré-

Men and Women Who
Made Paul's Ministry Team

Achaicus of Corinth (1 Cor. 16:17); Andronicus (Rom. 16:7); Aquila (Acts 18:18); Aristarchus (Acts 20:4; Col. 4:10); Artemas (Titus 3:12); Barnabas (Acts 13:2); Clement (Phil. 4:3); Crescens (2 Tim. 4:10); Demas (Col. 4:14; 2 Tim. 4:10); Epaphras (Col. 4:12); Epaphroditus (Phil. 2:25-30); Erastus (Acts 19:22; 2 Tim. 4:20); Euodia (Phil. 4:2-3); Fortunatus of Corinth (1 Cor. 16:17); Gaius of Corinth (Rom. 16:23); Gaius of Derbe (Acts 20:4); Jason (Rom. 16:21); Jesus Justus (Col. 4:11); John Mark (Acts 12:25; 13:13; Col. 4:10; 2 Tim. 4:11); Junia (Rom. 16:7); Lucius (Rom. 16:21); Luke (Col. 4:14; 2 Tim. 4:11); Mary of Rome (Rom. 16:6); Onesimus of Colosse (Col. 4:9; Philem. 10-18); Phoebe of Cenchrea (Rom. 16:1-2); Priscilla (Acts 18:18); Secundus of Thessalonica (Acts 20:4); Silas (Acts 15:40); Sopater of Berea (Acts 20:4); Sosipater (Rom. 16:21); Sosthenes (1 Cor. 1:1); Stephanas of Corinth (1 Cor. 16:17); Syntyche (Phil. 4:2-3); Tertius (Rom. 16:22); Timothy (Acts 16:1-3); Titus (2 Tim. 4:10); Trophimus of Ephesus (Acts 20:4; 21:29; 2 Tim. 4:20); Tychicus (Acts 20:4; Eph. 6:21; Col. 4:7; 2 Tim. 4:12); Urbanus (Rom. 16:9)

sumé. Just as a football running back recognizes the value of the offensive line blocking for him, so Paul realized there were many who helped him in ministry. He was always eager to give them the credit they deserved. Although he wrote in the first person in his various letters, in all but two he identified his partners in ministry before he addressed those to whom he was writing.

The tasks accomplished by those on Paul's ministry team were as varied as the members of the team itself. Each used unique gifts and abilities to effectively serve as part of the overall ministry team. When each member served out of his or her strength, the team was strong. In contrast, if one member of the team failed to do his or her part, the whole team suffered. Paul gathered those around him that would complement his ministry. This is one reason he is remembered today as the greatest missionary in the history of Christianity.

Some members of Paul's ministry team are better known than others. Barnabas was Paul's early mentor and recognized his ministry potential when other church leaders were not sure Paul was really a Christian (Acts 9:26-27). Some Bible teachers think Luke was instrumental in convincing Paul to launch his ministry into Europe (16:8-10). God used Aquila and Priscilla in a mentoring role in the life of another great preacher of the Early Church, Apollos (18:26). They also helped Paul in ministry, even as they worked together making tents (vv. 2-4).

Paul described Timothy as "my true son in the faith" (1 Tim. 1:2) and "my beloved son" (2 Tim. 1:2). He also described Titus as "my true son in our common faith" (Titus 1:4). Paul may have had a similar ministry in the life of Onesimus (Philem. 10).

Throughout his ministry, various individuals assisted Paul in his ministry by providing necessary financial support. While Paul was in Corinth, Timothy and Silas brought a much-needed financial gift from the churches in Macedonia to help underwrite the costs of his ministry (Acts 18:5; Phil. 4:15-16). Stephanas, Fortunatus, and Achaicus encouraged Paul by bringing a financial gift to the apostle after he had left Corinth (1 Cor. 16:17-18). Epaphroditus is also identified as one who brought Paul a financial gift from the church at Philippi (Phil. 4:18).

Other members of the team found their strength in practical acts of service. Tertius served Paul by assisting him in writing the Epistle to the Romans (16:22). Others, including Phoebe (vv. 1-2), Tychicus (Eph. 6:21), Onesimus (Col. 4:7-9), and Timothy (1 Thess. 3:2), carried Paul's Epistles to the various churches he wrote. Some churches Paul helped establish may have des-

ignated individuals from their church to join Paul's team and
serve in any capacity they could. Paul described Epaphroditus
as the messenger of the church at Philippi (2:25).

There is much we do not know about Paul's ministry
team. The group dynamics at work in his team may have
changed from time to time. Some of the men and women
identified as part of the team are known today only by their
name. But based on what we know, it appeared every member of the team had a function, and as they worked together,
great exploits were accomplished for God.

The Church as the Body of Christ

When Paul wrote his First Epistle to the church at Corinth,
he described that congregation as "the body of Christ"
(12:27). While many people use that expression today to
broadly describe the relationship between all Christians in the
world, Paul used it in the context of a local church. The ideas
of *the Body of Christ* and *team ministry* help us recognize the
importance of functioning as a cohesive team. Unfortunately,
the church at Corinth had many problems that needed to be
addressed, but the consistent emphasis of the entire Epistle
was that they unite together with common purpose and function as a healthy Body to serve Christ.

When writing the Romans from Corinth, Paul used the
body as a metaphor to recognize individuality within the local church. "We have many members within one body, but
all the members do not have the same function" (12:4). Some
people wrongly believe conformity is the key to church unity.
Paul taught the Corinthian church they should be united in
purpose of heart, while recognizing diversity among the
members in service (1 Cor. 12:12-31).

The diversity of the Body should encourage everyone to
find his or her place on the ministry team. Some Christians
believe they cannot serve God because they can't do ministry
like others. Paul reminded the Corinthians the foot is not
eliminated from the body because it is not a hand (v. 15). He
referred to other body parts to demonstrate that diversity was

necessary within a healthy Body. When a member fails to serve as God intended, the whole Body is disabled (v. 17).

While people have various reasons for not getting involved in ministry, Paul reminded the Corinthians that ultimately "God has set the members, each one of them, in the body just as He pleased" (v. 18). God uses job transfers, the spiritual needs of your family, the invitation to get involved, your interest in a particular church ministry, or your pastor's current preaching series to accomplish His purpose.

When we recognize we are part of Christ Body, we cannot ignore God's purpose in adding each member to the Body. "The eye cannot say to the hand, 'I have no need of you'; nor again the head to the feet, 'I have no need of you" (v. 21). Sometimes, the most important parts of our human body are those we notice least. The same phenomenon can be true within a local church (vv. 22-23). God needs everyone; God needs you.

While much of Paul's discussion of the church as a Body focuses on the role of individual church members, he was also careful to identify the supremacy of Christ in the local church. He described Christ as "the head of the body." One practical ramification of that title of Christ is "that in all things He may have the preeminence" (Col. 1:18). This view was not that of Paul alone. When addressing a particular problem in another church, the apostle John described the particular individual responsible for the problem as one "who loves to have the preeminence among them" (3 John 9).

The ultimate goal of the Body is that it functions in a healthy way. While many churches struggle to build a healthy spirit of fellowship in their church, Paul saw ministry as a key to creating strong relational bonds within a congregation. In his Epistle to the Ephesians, Paul described the Body as "joined and knit together by what every joint supplies, according to the effective working by which every part does its share." When the Body is healthy and functions as God intends, that "causes growth of the body for the edifying of itself in love" (4:16).

Spiritual Gifts and Team Ministry

As Paul described the local church as a Body, he often made reference to spiritual gifts. God has gifted every Christian in a unique way to more effectively serve Him. Paul viewed the existence of gifted Christians in local churches as an evidence of the work of Christ in their midst. Writing to the Corinthians, Paul noted, "The testimony of Christ was confirmed in you, so that you come short in no gift" (1 Cor. 1:6-7). Paul believed God had given that church enough members with their unique spiritual gifts to accomplish everything He wanted to do in their community through them. That's the same with your church.

Paul described spiritual gifts in three Epistles (Romans; 1 Corinthians; Ephesians). It is interesting that he provided a different list of gifts in each case. As he taught this principle in different churches, he probably referred to different gifts in each case because God had gifted different churches in different ways based on what He wanted to accomplish in those churches. As we look at our church today, our focus should not be on the gifts we may think are lacking but rather on those we have. The gifts God gives to different individuals and to churches reflect the kind of ministry He wants them to do.

Spiritual gifts equip Christians with the tools they need for effective outreach ministries. They also equip us with the ability to edify, encourage, and care for fellow believers (Eph. 4:12). Spiritual gifts provide the means by which Christians can experience their greatest personal fulfillment as they minister to others (Rom. 12:4-8).

Because God has given each of us a spiritual gift, He expects us to discover that gift, begin using it in ministry, and do what we can to develop it to its full potential. For many people, a spiritual gift inventory has proved an effective tool to help people discover areas in which they may be gifted. Your pastor will be able to recommend a particular gift inventory being widely used in your church or denomination so you can discover how God has gifted you for ministry.

As you seek to identify your spiritual gift(s), think also about the unique life experiences God has brought you through: your personal interests, passion for ministry, and the various skills you have learned over the years. Often, God uses these things blended together with an understanding of our unique spiritual giftedness to help us find our place on the ministry team.

Team Members Accountable

Paul understood that his modeling team ministry and teaching about the church as the Body of Christ would not be enough to insure the continued ministry of the team he developed in Corinth after his departure. He knew people do not always do what you expect. Rather, people tend to do what you inspect. That may be one reason why Paul organized the church in Corinth into small groups.

Personal Lessons to Take Away

1. One of the greatest privileges in life is being part of a ministry team that is planting a church.

2. I cannot do everything in ministry, so I must rely on others to help me in ministry as I assist them.

3. I will be more accountable in ministry when I am part of a ministry team.

4. I recognize the unity of the Body of Christ when I serve with others in a ministry team.

5. I will grow in character and spirituality when I become a part of a ministry team, and in return, I will help others grow in Christ.

Church Lessons to Take Away

1. Church planting will be more effective when ministry teams made up of many Christians who represent many spiritual gifts are involved in beginning the church.

2. Churches will develop the character and spirituality of

their members by involving them in church planting ministry teams.

3. Churches planted by an effective ministry team tend to be stronger, and their future tends to be more secure.

4. After a church is planted by a ministry team, it will remain strong by the continual ministry of cell groups, also called home Bible classes.

Personal Projects

Paul's ministry in Corinth did not take on any real significance until the arrival of others on his team. He recognized God had prepared each team member to make a unique contribution to the broader ministry of the team itself. He trained the various churches he influenced to organize into small groups to hold one another accountable. That was the only way each would become all God intended them to be. Now it's time for us to put the Book of Acts back into action.

1. The key to effective ministry in the Early Church was team ministry. Paul ministered as part of a ministry team. When he established new churches, it was clear God intended them to act as an effective ministry team. Evaluate your own reasons for not being part of the team. As you deal with attitudes that may be hindering your personal ministry effectiveness, begin looking for places you can help better serve your church or you can help plant a new church.

2. Have you found your place on the ministry team in your local church? God has gifted you with ability for a special ministry only you can do. As you consider your passion for ministry and various experiences God has introduced into your life, look for ministry patterns that reflect God's will for your life. Take time to reflect on how God has used you in the past to determine how He may use you in the future. Talk with your pastor or a spiritual Christian who will help you through this process. Then find a place where you can begin serving God. When you do that, the whole Body becomes just a little stronger.

3. Are you part of a small group in your church? Paul

warned that one could become "weary while doing good" (Gal. 6:9). You need a group that will encourage you to continue when you get tired. If you are not already part of a small group in your church, talk to your pastor about joining one this week.

Church Project

Divide the ministry team into smaller groups. Get each small group involved in assessment and information gathering that will strengthen the daughter church plant.

1. Divide the mother church into sections, and assign the small groups for the ministry team to each section in the mother church.

2. The sections can be adult Sunday School classes, ladies' groups, men's groups, ushers, board(s), and so forth.

3. Each small group is asked to survey (have conversations with, ask questions, listen to) each section of the mother church.

4. The purpose of surveying the mother church sections is to discover attitudes, opinions, feelings, and fears about the daughter church plant.

5. Each small group will ask questions about location, finances, name, worship type, strategy for planting, leadership, and so forth.

6. The purpose is to find out what the grass roots of the mother church is thinking about the daughter church plant. There is strength in knowledge; it makes for accurate plans, bold faith, and confidence.

7. Each small group will repeat its finds back to the ministry team the following week. Out of this research may come (positive or negative):
   - Revised prayer requests
   - Revised schedule of activities
   - Revised budget formulation
   - Revised vision or ministry statement
   - Revised strategy

12 | Building People Who Build People

The Ephesian Church

Toward the end of Paul's second missions trip, he stopped briefly in Ephesus. He visited "the synagogue and reasoned with the Jews" (Acts 18:19). Their initial response to Paul's message was apparently positive. Unlike the hostile reaction he had experienced from the Jews in other cities, these "asked him to stay a longer time with them" (v. 20). Unfortunately, Paul couldn't stay in Ephesus. He did, however, agree to return at his earliest convenience.

Later that year (A.D. 54), Paul began his third missionary journey. He traveled overland through Asia Minor, "strengthening all the disciples" (v. 23). From there, Paul made his way toward Ephesus to fulfill his promise to return. He remained in Ephesus longer than he stayed in any other city, making Ephesus his ministry base and his most effective anywhere. The key to his ministry success in Ephesus involved developing leaders, building up people who built up other people. In the process, Paul trained a new generation of Christian leaders.

The Conversion of John's Disciples

Paul's emphasis on leadership development in Ephesus began when he converted the disciples of John the Baptist to Christ. John the Baptist's success is described in the Gospels as large crowds gathered to hear him preach. John's ministry was multiplied by gathering disciples around him; he then sent them out to preach his message in other places. History records many disciples preached the message of John the Baptist well into the third century.

Shortly after Paul arrived in Ephesus, he met 12 men who

turned out to be disciples of John. They were preaching a message similar to John the Baptist prior to the baptism of Jesus. When Paul asked them about the Holy Spirit, they claimed they did not even know there was a Holy Spirit.

As Paul talked further with these men, it became clear they were receptive to teaching about the Messiah. But they had never believed in Jesus as their Messiah. Paul explained, "John indeed baptized with a baptism of repentance, saying to the people that they should believe on Him who would come after him, that is, on Christ Jesus" (Acts 19:4). When the men heard this, they accepted Jesus as the Christ and submitted to Christian baptism. Then Paul laid his hands on them and "the Holy Spirit came upon them, and they spoke with tongues and prophesied" (v. 6). Another "Gentile Pentecost"!

The Scriptures are not clear what these men did following their conversion. These 12 men may have also remained with Paul briefly to get a better understanding of the gospel and all its implications. It is reasonable to assume they continued their itinerate ministry with a more complete message.

Moving into the School of Tyrannus

Paul continued ministering in the synagogue in Ephesus for about three months, "reasoning and persuading concerning the things of the kingdom of God" (19:8). Once again, the Jews' response was mixed. While some believed, others rejected Paul's message and became antagonistic toward the gospel. Paul responded to this challenge by leaving the synagogue and meeting in a different location as he had done in Corinth. This time, the church moved to the school of Tyrannus.

The Greek word *scholē* refers to the lecture hall or room used by a philosopher or orator. Such halls were extremely common at that time in most Greek cities. Bible teachers believe this was the school of the sophist named Tyrannus mentioned by Suidas. This facility was made available to Paul to teach the gospel. Others believe this was the private synagogue of a Jewish rabbi named Tyrannus who was sympathetic to the preaching of Paul. Still others believe the expression "school of Tyrannus" was the name of a public hall named in honor of the original owner. The church simply rented the facilities for its ministry.

Paul's ministry at this school continued daily for two years "so that all who dwelt in Asia heard the word of the Lord Jesus, both Jews and Greeks" (v. 10). This approach to ministry marked a departure from previous methodology used by Paul and may be viewed as a new evangelistic strategy. According to an early Syrian text of this passage, Paul taught the Scriptures daily from 11 A.M. through 4 P.M. Those who heard him apparently communicated the content of Paul's teaching to others in Ephesus and in other cities. Using this method, Paul trained those who in turn went to other smaller communities to establish new churches. The churches in Colosse, Smyrna, Pergamos, Thyatira, Sardis, Philadelphia, and Laodicea (Rev. 2—3) were probably established during this period of time.

Because he focused on leadership training, Paul continued to have a broader ministry in Ephesus. During this period, his ministry was also marked by a number of "unusual miracles" (Acts 19:11). There were occasions when people were healed and demons cast out. So spectacular were these and other miracles that soon some outside the Christian community attempted to duplicate them.

Many Jews recognized the reality of demon possession but relied on the Jewish rite of exorcism to cast them out of a possessed person. When a group of itinerate Jewish exorcists came to Ephesus, a situation arose that gave great spiritual impetus to the church. Seven sons of a Jewish chief priest named Sceva attempted to practice their rite of exorcism with near disastrous results. When they addressed the demon "by the Jesus whom Paul preaches" (v. 13), the demon responded, "Jesus I know, and Paul I know; but who are you?" (v. 15). The demon-possessed man then turned on the seven exorcists and overpowered them. The men fled from the house naked and wounded, grateful they were still alive.

A Citywide Revival

Naturally, reports of this event spread quickly through the city of Ephesus, and the people were overcome with fear "and the name of the Lord Jesus was magnified" (v. 17). This event shocked many believers into a renewed understanding of the spirit world and its influence in the occult religions of the day. Many confessed their own involvement in these practices, and as an act of repentance, they brought the books they owned that they had used in these practices "and burned them in the sight of all" (v. 19). The total value of the books destroyed at that time was estimated at "fifty thousand pieces of silver." A "piece of silver" mentioned here referred to a day's wage for a common laborer. In today's economy the total value of the books destroyed was about a quarter million dollars. This response among believers resulted in continued spiritual and numerical growth in the church. "So the word of the Lord grew mightily and prevailed" (v. 20).

At the height of the Ephesian Revival, Paul determined to return to Macedonia and Achaia before going to Jerusalem. Even as he made those plans, Paul had his sights set on a new goal. He began telling others of his plan, always adding, "After I have been there, I must also see Rome" (v. 21). Throughout his missionary career, Paul consistently sought out the principal cities and made them the objects of his evangelistic efforts. It was only natural that sooner or later he would look to the largest city of the world as a mission field. He knew that if the gospel were preached in Rome, it would quickly be spread throughout the entire empire.

Paul sent Timothy and Erastus on ahead, probably to prepare for his ministry in Greece, while he remained in Ephesus. He had already told the Corinthians he was planning to send Timothy ahead (1 Cor. 16:10). Of the other members of his team, Erastus was the most logical choice. He was a native of Corinth and once held a civic office in the city (Rom. 16:23). Together the two worked their way through Greece, ministering to the churches and preparing them for Paul's visit.

Although Paul intended to remain in Ephesus until Pentecost (1 Cor. 16:8), a situation arose that probably cut his stay short. The evangelistic efforts of the church were so successful that the silver industry in the city was beginning to suffer a financial setback. Much of this industry was devoted to making silver shrines used in the worship of Diana. It did not take long for those losing money to recognize the relationship between the drop in sales and Paul's evangelistic zeal. At a meeting of the silversmith guild, one craftsman named Demetrius noted, "This Paul has persuaded and turned away many people, saying that they are not gods which are made with hands, so not only is this trade of ours in danger of falling into disrepute, but also the temple of the great goddess of Diana may be despised and her magnificence destroyed, whom all Asia and the world worship" (Acts 19:26-27).

The worship of Diana was the chief religious practice of the city of Ephesus. According to their myths, Diana was "born" in the woods near Ephesus at the site of her temple when her image fell down from the heavens. She was viewed as the mother earth god and was usually portrayed as a multi-breasted goddess. Her temple in Ephesus was not considered her home but rather the chief shrine where she could and should be worshiped. The silver shrines made by Demetrius and his colleagues were probably crude copies of the temple that were normally purchased by pilgrims and carried home as worship aids in the cult.

Paul's success in evangelism meant the silversmiths were losing pilgrims to the temple and, therefore, experiencing dwindling sales. The burning of occult books probably shocked Demetrius and the others into recognizing the decline of their trade was more than a passing phase. If the Christians continued to be successful in their evangelism efforts, it would not be long before the magnificent temple would be obsolete.

The group became incensed and began chanting loudly, "Great is Diana of the Ephesians" (v. 28). In the confusion that followed, most of the city filled the public theater (it seated over 30,000; the ruins are still observable), but most of them did not even know why they were there. Somewhere in the rush, two of Paul's companions from Macedonia, Gaius and Aristarchus, were seized by the mob and taken into the theater. Paul wanted to join his friends, but his disciples and sympathetic public officials convinced him to remain outside.

In the midst of the confusion, the Jews appointed Alexander as their spokesman to address the crowd. But when he began to address the group, they once again broke out in the chant, "Great is Diana of the Ephesians!" (v. 34). The chanting continued in the public theater for about two hours. Only then was the city clerk able to gain control of the meeting and address the crowd. He argued no one was disputing the greatness of their beloved goddess and warned them that such uprisings could result in the unwanted involvement of Rome in their civic affairs. He noted that if Demetrius and the other silversmiths had a legitimate concern, the issue could be addressed by open courts and officials.

By the time the riot ended, Paul realized he had once again become the center of a controversy that threatened the church. He called the Christians together and revealed his plan to leave. After he embraced those with whom he spent a long time, he left the city and began his planned tour of Greece. Paul had preached in Ephesus longer than he had preached in any other city. He could leave without being overly concerned for the future of this church. Because of his ministry based in the School of Tyrannus, he had trained a generation of leaders capable of carrying on the ministry he had begun. Not long after, one of Paul's partners in ministry, Timothy, would return to Ephesus to pastor this significant church.

Paul's Pattern for Leadership Training

Early in his ministry, Paul described his evangelistic goal "to preach the gospel, not where Christ was named, lest I should build on another man's foundation" (Rom. 15:20). The last reference to Paul's ministry in the Acts describes him as "preaching the kingdom of God and teaching the things concerning the Lord Jesus Christ with all confidence, no one forbidding him" (28:31). Paul stayed true to his evangelistic calling, using every available resource at every available time to reach every available person for Christ. Evangelism always had a high priority in his personal ministry.

"And the things that you have heard from me among many witnesses, commit these to faithful men who will be able to teach others also" (2 Tim. 2:2).

But Paul also understood he was not immortal. Sooner or later, he, too, would pass from the scene. His departure appeared close on the horizon. Because he was committed to preaching the gospel widely, Paul also committed himself to training others to carry on the ministry of the local church he planted. Developing new leaders was an integral part of Paul's evangelistic strategy to reach the whole world for Christ.

In a day when men learned a trade by apprenticing with their father or another tradesman, Paul gathered young men around him who could see him do ministry. In this mentoring relationship, Paul involved these men in various aspects of the ministry to mature their ministry skills. He might send some ahead to another city to prepare for his coming or leave others behind to continue ministering in a new church as he moved on. In the process, a new generation of leaders was given the opportunity to grow and develop under his tutelage.

Even when the men he trained were mature enough to launch out into ministry on their own, Paul continued sharing with them the insights of his experience. The Pastoral Epistles of 1 and 2 Timothy and Titus reflect his ongoing leadership training efforts in their lives. His letters were written to encourage men in their ongoing ministry, answer specific concerns, and guide them in various aspects of their ministry.

It is in his Second Epistle to Timothy that Paul discussed the nature of his ministry at the School of Tyrannus. He reminded Timothy of "the things that you have heard from me among many witnesses" (2 Tim. 2:2*a*). While Timothy accompanied Paul throughout much of his second and third mission trips, many Bible teachers believe this allusion has particular reference to Paul's ministry in Ephesus where Timothy was then pastoring. The availability of the hall provided Paul a unique opportunity to accelerate his leadership-training ministry. As people were converted to Christ during that revival, many apparently reflected leadership potential. Also, as new churches were established throughout Asia, potential leaders may have moved to Ephesus to learn from Paul. What Paul had done informally for years, he did in a more formal context in Ephesus. While we know the names of Timothy, Titus, Epaphras, and a few others that were probably part of that group, there were apparently many others whose names have since been forgotten.

Developing leaders was not an end in itself as far as Paul was concerned. He wanted his students to invest their lives into others. "Commit these to faithful men who will be able to teach others also" (2 Tim. 2:2*b*). He wanted Timothy to be involved in the ministry of building up people who would build up other people. The apostle understood a successful leadership development ministry would set in motion an unending chain for generations to come. As long as church leaders could find people with potential, there would always be a fresh group of new leaders.

The key to success in this plan was recognizing leadership potential. Many church leaders struggle with this today. Those interested in this aspect of ministry suggest many things to look for in a potential leader. Sometimes the thing a pastor in one church looks for may be different from another pastor. While natural or learned abilities are an important part of any ministry, Paul looked for one thing even more important—*faithfulness*.

Above all, character counts! There are books and courses widely available to teach various ministry skills and methodology, but if the student is not faithful in his or her studies, faithful in applying the lessons learned, and faithful in con-

tinuing to serve in good times and bad, that student will
never rise to a position of leadership. In the event an un-
faithful person is appointed to a church office, it is usually
not long before those responsible regret their actions. Paul
warned Timothy not to appoint novices to leadership positions (1 Tim. 3:6) but to give people time to be tested before
they were appointed to offices (v. 10).

What God Looks For in a Leader!

While Paul saw *faithfulness* as the key to leadership potential, he had other things he looked for before entrusting leadership to various individuals. In his First Epistle to Timothy,
Paul listed several qualifications for deacons. Those that
would assume this office were each expected to have a reverence toward life, control his tongue, practice self-discipline
by being "not given to much wine, not greedy for money,"
know and apply the faith to one's personal lifestyle, be recognized as blameless, have a good relationship with his wife
and children, and have the heart of a servant (3:8-10, 12-13).

Paul also had standards he looked for in women involved in
ministry. He insisted they "be reverent, not slanderers, temper-
ate, faithful in all things" (v. 11). Many Bible teachers believe
Paul is referring to the wives of deacons in this description.
Others teach he is talking about any woman involved in any
aspect of ministry. The characteristics listed for deacons and
the women are noble ideals to be pursued by all Christians.

Paul also had a list of qualifications he looked for before
endorsing someone as a pastor. Paul shared these standards
with Timothy and Titus to help them in their respective
ministries (1 Tim. 3:1-7; Titus 1:5-9). In total, Paul identifies
20 qualities including (1) irreproachable, (2) the husband of
one wife, (3) sober, (4) wise, (5) sociable, (6) hospitable, (7)
teachable, (8) not given to wine, (9) not arrogant, (10) slow
to anger, (11) not violent, (12) peaceful, (13) conciliatory,
(14) unselfish, (15) a good leader in his family, (16) well liked
by outsiders, (17) upright, (18) just, (19) holy, and (20) not a
new convert.

Personal Lessons to Take Away

1. God expects me to grow in character and ministry skills so I can serve Him.

2. I can be trained for Christian leadership in my church.

3. I must learn to mentor others as I minister for God and work in the church.

4. I must be aware of spiritual opposition to the work of my church and in my personal Christian life.

5. There will always be those who want to serve God with "good works," but some may not be saved, and they need my instruction in the gospel.

Church Lessons to Take Away

1. When planting a new church, it is important to develop a program to teach potential members biblical character and equip them for personal ministry.

2. Success in a new church is tied to the effectiveness of training new members to do the work of ministry.

3. When planting a new church, give attention to developing and teaching a team who can help in starting the new church.

4. When beginning a new church, give the members a vision of church planting so they can begin praying, planning, and working toward another church plant after or while the new church is established.

Personal Projects

Jesus asked His disciples to "pray the Lord of the harvest to send out laborers into His harvest" (Matt. 9:38). Many believe Jesus' command is a challenge and pattern for us today, because "the harvest truly is plentiful, but the laborers are few" (v. 37).

Now it is your turn. What are you doing about the shortage of workers in your church? Will you pray that God will provide what is needed? That's a good start, but remember, God enlists workers from those who pray. As you pray, use the following suggestions to help you decide your next step:

1. Evaluate your own reasons for not being a leader. Remember, the key to recognizing leadership potential is faithfulness. Look for something you can do as part of the ministry team in your church, and do it faithfully.

2. In the section *What God Looks For in a Leader!* reference is made to several lists of desirable qualities in Scripture. As you consider your own involvement as a leader in your church, use one of these lists as your Personal Leadership Inventory. How do you measure up? As you look over the list, identify your strengths and weaknesses. You can become a better leader by building on your strengths while addressing the weaknesses that may hold you back.

3. Effective leaders are always growing. As you evaluate your strengths and weaknesses, take time to develop a personal leadership training strategy. Is there a book you need to read or a course to take to better equip you for a particular ministry? You may want to make an appointment with your pastor to ask him to mentor you as Paul mentored others. As your church starts a new church, there will be a need for leaders in both the mother and daughter church. What do you think God wants you to do to help meet that need?

Church Project

Mentoring course. Even before your church plants a new church, make plans for a course of study to mentor the planting team. Use the following questions to get started:

1. Who are candidates to direct and organize the mentoring course of study? _____

   _____.

2. Who are candidates to teach the mentoring course of study? _____

   _____.

3. Can the mentoring course of study begin before the actual plant? Yes _____ No _____. Why? _____
_____.

4. Suggested mentoring courses of study. Appoint someone to study and be ready to teach:
   - Hybels, Bill. *Art of Self Leadership.* www.willowcreek.org
   - Maxwell, John. *Joshua's Men.* www.injoy.com
   - Woodruff, Sid. (Southern Baptist) *Drawing Men to God: Men's Ministry.* LifeWay Church Resources.

5. Suggested mentoring books. Appoint someone to read and be ready to teach:
   - Anderson, Leith. *Leadership That Works.* Bethany House, 220 pages
   - Barna, George. *Leaders on Leadership.* Regal, 324 pages
   - Maxwell, John. *21 Indispensable Qualities of a Leader.* Thomas Nelson, 157 pages
   - ————. *Developing the Leader Within You.* Thomas Nelson, 178 pages
   - ————. *Developing the Leaders Around You.* Thomas Nelson, 215 pages
   - Towns, Elmer. *The 8 Laws of Leadership,* Church Growth Institute, 91 pages
   - ————. *The Successful Christian Life.* www.elmertowns.com
   - Towns, Ruth. *Women Gifted for Ministry.* Thomas Nelson, 160 pages